AUTISM AND US

OLD AS TIME

A Social History of Autism

EUSTACIA CUTLER

author of *A Thorn in My Pocket*

Autism and Us: Old As Time

All marketing and publishing rights guaranteed to and reserved by:

FUTURE HORIZONSINC.

(817) 277-0727
(817) 277-2270 (fax)
E-mail: info@fhautism.com
www.fhautism.com

© 2022 Eustacia Cutler

ISBN: 9781949177909

For my children and my children's children

CONTENTS

INTRODUCTION

The animal world is full of anomalies: white elephants and seven toed cats. They don't disturb the order of life; in fact, they rather enhance it. We humans, too, have our white haired young and those born with extra toes. We also have anomalies like tone deafness and color blindness. But none of them upset the social order of life as do those born with the anomaly of autism. Though they look the same as we do and their toes and fingers count the same, their behavior can be so astonishingly peculiar that it's all we can do not to react like the Duchess in Lewis Carroll's *Alice in Wonderland*.

Speak roughly to your little boy,
And beat him when he sneezes:
He only does it to annoy,
Because he knows it teases.

Even though we know that speaking roughly won't work any more than beating will help the Duchess with her little boy—even though we've learned enough bio-neurology to understand how animal instinct accounts for much of our behavior—none of it stops us from wanting to behave like the Duchess. We haven't as much free will as we like to think we have; and coming to terms with that reality is hard, particularly where there's autism.

* * * *

Like all warm blooded animals, we raise and teach our young, love, scheme, bond and remember. While other animals run in packs, gaggles, and herds, we humans run in tribes. We're also symbiotic with those other animals. I looked up "symbiosis" in Noah Webster's Dictionary; and he defines it as "the living together in intimate association of two dissimilar organisms." Yes, that's us. We share our lives with cats and dogs; we use eye contact and vocal sounds to make our wants known to one another; we're each aware when the other is happy or sad. In a word we gain benefit—even survival—from each other. In addition, symbiosis can induce baby animals from other species to pick up behavior patterns from humans. The African tale *Born Free* tells of Elsa the orphaned lion cub, who bonds with the couple who rescue her and has to be actively taught by them how to leave the human nest and behave like a lion in the wild.

Symbiosis between humans and animals also turns up in everyday domestic ways: witness my life with the blue jays in the wild garden around my house. The jays nested in the old wisteria vines and policed the property. When Simpkin, our tabby cat, went on the prowl after the sparrows, the jays would set up an alert cry quite different from their usual jay talk. I'd run out, grab Simpkin, and the jays would return to their usual caws. Were they signaling me or was it just a general alert? The sparrows didn't pay attention; I did.

The symbiotic give-and-take between animals can be more gracious and far-reaching than we give the animals credit for.

When the going gets tough, it allows the lesser animal to back off unharmed. In the wild, too long a stare is understood as a challenge. The lesser animal must concede to the alpha animal or expect a fight. Lesser animals won't fight if they can withdraw with their dignity and needs intact, a conciliatory role that diplomats carry out for nations.

This conciliatory role played out for the squirrel that came into my kitchen one time looking for treats. Our introduction to each other had begun earlier when the squirrel took to feasting on the bird seed I'd put on the outside windowsill. The birds had already established a pecking order. Jays first, and what bird seed was left the sparrows could have. Then the squirrel took over. He was bolder than jays and sparrows, but only up to a point.

It was Saturday and I was unloading a week's worth of groceries from the car, running up the stone steps to the kitchen, dumping the first load on the kitchen floor and running back for the next one. I returned with it, only to find that the squirrel had come in the kitchen window pushed open a paper bag of cookies and was about to help himself. We stared at each other. It felt like an eternity. Because of the height of the stone steps we were literally eyeball to eyeball. I knew that if I frightened the squirrel, he might run in a panic through the house. Simpkin the cat was a fierce hunter, and Henry the dog would be only too happy to join him. The squirrel knew that I was the alpha animal. Since the cookies were mine and the territory was mine, retreat would be better than mayhem and murder. Not taking his eyes off me, he backed away from the bag of cookies and made for the kitchen counter—not in a frightened scamper, but in the squirrel equivalent of a slow walk at high noon. Then he hopped up on the counter and out the window. He left with his dignity intact, keeping me at bay with his "high noon" walk, what the Chinese call "saving face."

In the long moment when the squirrel and I stared at each other, we each had to put the scene together alone and decide how to act on it. The squirrel had to swallow his greed, retire with dignity, and hope that he could still feast off the sunflower seeds (not as good as cookies but always there in winter). I had to give the squirrel time for that escape rather than have my lamps overturned, my curtains torn to shreds, and a mangled squirrel body to bury. Embedded in each of our neurology was a mutual need for peaceful living, and embedded in that mutual need is a tiny scrap of free will: the tap root of civilization.

Most readers today are too young to have lived through the 1950s: a decade when we were in a Cold War with Russia. The tension it created produced the McCarthy Hearings: Senator McCarthy was seeking to penalize prominent figures who he deemed were—or had been—card-carrying Communists. Among those under his investigative thumb was Robert Oppenheimer who'd been part of the atomic bomb project. During the hearing process, Oppenheimer told a friend that he'd found himself riding in the elevator alone with McCarthy, each staring at the other.

"Oh my God! What'd you do?"

"I winked."

Most creatures under stress would not be able to summon the conciliatory grace of Oppenheimer. And some creatures are not necessarily kind.

One fall afternoon in the 1930s when I was a child, my mother was sitting on the steps of our porch and a hungry squirrel came up to her looking for food. Whether my aunt whose house we'd inherited had fed the squirrel, I don't know, but whatever the past, my mother opened her hands to show she had nothing to give. The squirrel saw her empty hands, sprang onto her head, dug its sharp claws into her cheek leaving a long bloody vengeful scratch, and sprang off—never to return.

The difference between the vengeful squirrel and Lewis Carroll's Duchess is that the vengeful squirrel had no way to justify its fury; it could only attack and flee. The Duchess can justify hers.

Over and over she can speak severely to her boy and beat him when he sneezes:

For he can thoroughly enjoy
the pepper when he pleases.

What if her boy can't enjoy it? What if he hates pepper and has no way to justify *his* feelings? Or even understand them? What if he's autistic and is missing the symbiosis that connects the animal world? Do you wonder that he's anxious? That he "acts out"? He doesn't even know what "acting out" means. Faced with a lack he has no way to understand—all his tiny scrap of free will can summon is a burst of meaningless chaotic energy, known in the autism world as a "meltdown."

And the chaos that meltdown creates makes us so anxious that all our scrap of free will can do is sweep our confused, angry, shame-filled feelings under the carpet.

Time to lift up the carpet and have a look.

That sounds like a good idea until I try to do it, only to find I'm up against human ambiguity. Autism is imprecise, and so are we. Autism exists on a spectrum, and so do we. Who decides when to call an eccentricity a disorder? Who benefits from the decision? And how? I find I'm writing a literary mongrel. Not even a half breed, but a mix of what I've lived, witnessed, read in novels and textbooks, and listened to at conferences: part memoir, part social history and cautionary tale, part opinion, gossip, and a bit of spontaneous fiction. I finally decided it was the only way to bring to life the forgotten past when those with autism struggled to survive in a world that called them "changelings" and declared them "not human."

I also decided that the best way to understand that past was to begin with the present, but again I stumbled into ambiguity. Every animal belongs to a species, but each animal differs a little from the rest of its species. I was up against an old truth I first learned when I had to dissect a frog in freshman biology. We were each given a formaldehyde frog and a printed frog diagram with arrows pointing to different body parts. We were told to dissect our frog and draw a picture. I studied the diagram, dissected the frog, and looked for the body parts. They were there alright, but they didn't look quite like the diagram, and they weren't quite where the arrows pointed. As I drew the required picture, it dawned on me that my frog was uniquely itself.

So when you read what follows, keep that frog in mind and think of my words as a series of diagrams with arrows indicating what to look for. Also bear with me when I call a person "autistic." I know I should say "on the autism spectrum." Or, as professionals put it: "Autism Spectrum Disorder," often shortened to ASD. But try using that phase when telling a story. I've also found that the term "ASD" does not please those diagnosed with the variety of autism called "Asperger." Though professional lingo puts them under the "ASD" banner, they resent it. They relish their "Aspie" moniker and have no intention of letting it go.

Again the frog rule applies, even to the naming of things.

2

THE NATURE OF AUTISM

Asa and Arthur look like any other pair of bright seven-year-olds.
Then after a bit, you become conscious of an old fashioned, well
mannered remoteness about them, as if they have escaped from a
Victorian ghost yarn dreamed up before there was electricity. Like
the computers they love too much, they're good at memory and
logic. They could read by the time they were three, but they still
play at the level of solitary five-year-olds. As yet they have no gift
for making friends, a relationship they hunger for.

Asa, blond and stout with no muscle tone, was non verbal his
first six months in a special class. He could only communicate
with his teacher by acting out charades. A year later, now fluent
with language, he uses elaborate verbal arguments to fend off his
anxiety over the lacks in himself that he doesn't understand. Today
he is explaining to his teacher, logical point by logical point, why he
does not like to have paint or sand touch his hands. Logic is Asa's
brand of control.

Arthur is thin and pale with great grey circles under his eyes.
He has a problem with things that make him feel sad, so much
so he can't even say the word. Instead he says "das," which is
"sad' spelt backward, and then he laughs. Laughter is his brand of
control. Arthur loves to watch the auto races on TV, but recently

he was "das" when a famous racing car driver drove his car off the track and was killed. So he dug a hole in the garden and buried his cloth "Piglet" in it. Arthur's mother said Piglet wasn't dead and helped him dig Piglet up. Asa told Arthur he could explain death to him because he'd read *Charlotte's Web*. But Arthur knew better than both of them. He laughed.

Today Arthur and Asa are playing with Mike who's five and non verbal. Mike has trouble understanding the give-and-take of games, even a simple game like tag. He doesn't understand that one person is "it" and chases another person till he "tags" him. Then that person is "it" and chases and tags a third person. But Mike can only careen wildly around the room alone. So in order to introduce him to the idea of games—and with the help of a teacher who is guiding all three into the fellowship of friends— Asa and Arthur invent a game they call "Chase Mike." It goes like this: Mike runs around the room pretending he's driving a car, Asa and Arthur chase after him. No tagging, just a chase. Suddenly, in the midst of the wild careening the game creates, Mike takes an unintended spill. The teacher, improvising to the game spirit, calls out: "Help! Quick! Mike's had an accident! We must drive him to the hospital!" She makes siren sounds: "Eeeennnnnnnneeeeooo! Eeennnnnneeeeeeoooo!"

Asa and Arthur catch on and join in. Everybody gets Mike to the hospital; they stretch him out on the floor. Mike likes this game—he's seen it on TV. He plays it to the hilt and lies stiff as a board. Arthur grabs up two Lego blocks and plunks them on Mike's chest. "Kaa-chung!" He makes the heart resuscitator sound and jumps back. "Kaa-chung!" He, too, has seen it on TV. "That's it!" says the teacher, "You're saving Mike, you're getting his heart going." Arthur shakes his head. "No, he's dead." He leans over and closes Mike's eyes, then stands back and laughs. It's too "das" to bear.

Arthur understands the ritual of death, the closing of eyes, and the burial of a body. These are observable actions. But the idea that his adored racing car driver is gone: gone where? That a beloved someone has suddenly disappeared and there's a body laid out in a box heaped with flowers can make the best of us want to go up to that body and shake it awake. But for Arthur, death is an absence he has no way to comprehend. The closest he can come to it is "das." For him, "das" is something so troubling and anxiety making that he has to spell the word backwards, as if he could turn that something around and make it un-happen. His other solution is to laugh.

All three boys enjoy imitating the death ceremonies they've seen on TV, but when Arthur closes Mike's eyes he knows Mike will shortly open his eyes and spring up. Even Piglet buried in the garden can be dug up and brought back to life. Does he take in the finality of death?

Chimpanzee expert Jane Goodall tells of a mother chimp carrying her dead baby chimp around with her till finally she accepts death's reality. Is she grieving for her loss? Does she know her baby's body is in a state of decay? Or is it both? Elephants know when and where members of their herd have died; they return to mourn over their remains. I recall an old cat I loved who sensed death was approaching and took refuge in the closet to die. But as far as we know, we humans are the only species to be fully aware that in time death will overtake us. And as far as we can tell, Arthur does not know that.

Arthur can only anticipate the future in terms of what he's already experienced. If yesterday's loud school bell has upset him, today he'll anticipate it—growing more anxious as the clock hands approach the time when the bell rang yesterday. If a new situation crops up, he will respond with an action he's taken before (or seen on TV). Whether or not it suits what's happened, it's all he has.

But the future is fast approaching when he'll be too old for a class where they play "Chase Mike," and will need our help in planning for it.

* * * *

Twenty years ago, when Nicholas, my youngest grandson, was a baby just starting to talk, the first word I heard him say wasn't "Mama" or "Dada" but "Oreo." He looked at us, he pointed to the cookie jar and he said "Oreo." We all laughed, it was so unexpected, but I knew that each step in a bio-neurological gift we take for granted had developed fully.

Step 1: Conceptual Thinking. Nicholas understood the *idea* of a cookie: what it is and what it's for. A cookie is sweet and crunchy and it's for eating.

Conceptual thinking eludes Arthur. You can ask him to point to a shovel, and he can point to it, he can name it. But if you ask him to point to the thing you dig with, he's lost. He doesn't get the *idea* of a shovel: what it is and what it's for. That means he has no way to understand that his little sand shovel and his father's snow shovel are both shovels; that the backhoe digging a hole in the garden for a swimming pool is also a shovel. The result is he can't generalize. Understanding shovels doesn't matter much, but here's a generalization that I ran into in New York City that matters a lot. An autistic young man has learned that he should cross the street he lives on only when the traffic light is green. When it's red, he must wait till it turns green again.

Since he can't generalize, he can't understand that this general rule applies to all red and green traffic lights on all streets. Though he's highly intelligent, he cannot negotiate new traffic lights and travels only the streets where he's memorized the lights. Explaining won't work, any more than explaining blindness to a blind man will give him sight.

Step 2: Context. Nicholas also understood that he was sitting in his highchair, the place where he gets things to eat. If he wanted a cookie, he better ask for it quick before someone takes him out of that place. He already understood location and how it relates to what happens.

Arthur, like many autistics, has trouble with context. He doesn't understand prepositions like "over," "under," "around": words that relate to the position of one object or person to another. Temple had this trouble. She finally grasped the meaning of "under" when the 1950s "cold-war" air raid drill bell rang, and the class had to get *under* the teacher's long table at the head of the room. It took the physical act of getting under the table before she could grasp the meaning of the word "under." Context also applies to "relevance," i.e., the relationship of one *idea* to another. That's even harder for autistics to grasp (more on this later.)

Step 3: Shared Information. When Nicholas pointed to the cookie jar, he looked at *us* not at the cookie jar. He understood that we had a different mind from his and he needed to get the idea of a cookie from his mind into ours. Arthur doesn't understand that others have thoughts that are different from his. Though he knows his own mind, he's unaware of ours. Basic to shared information is eye contact. Mothers look at babies and babies look back. Though Arthur can describe every detail he can see in the room, he doesn't look at you when you look at him. The social connection of eye contact escapes him. Clinical studies on infant eye response show that babies respond to human eyes, even to the big eyes of a rag doll.

Step 4: Executive Function. Nicholas could put these three steps together and act on them. Sounds easy? Not really. Think of it like a basketball player getting the ball into the basket. He has to coordinate his intention and the spot where he is on the basketball court (context) with his eye/hand coordination. At the same time he has to use his body to dodge his opponents, signal his teammates, and get to the spot where he can toss the ball into the basket. Putting all that together and acting on it is no slam dunk.

Now think of Arthur, who doesn't fully grasp the idea of a basketball game and how its layout (context) determines the action of the players. Nor can he understand that teamwork is a form of shared information. Given those lacks, what does he have to put together and act on? Not what Nicholas has, that's for sure. Fortunately, what he does have is memory and logic. His favorite TV show is *Jeopardy*, which uses both. But *Jeopardy* depends on information that has already happened. The information Nicholas is sharing with us is in the process of happening and isn't necessarily logical. It's a "feeling" exchange, not a "thinking" exchange.

To clarify the difference between these two exchanges, I turned to two experts: Neuroscientist Antonio Damasio and Simon Baron Cohen, professor of developmental psychopathology. I was lucky enough to hear Damasio speak at the New York 92nd Street YMJA. Awed by his insight and know-how, I wrote down these words as he said them:

"We are not thinking beings who feel we are feeling beings who think. The mind is in the service of the [neurological] body."

To gain more detailed information, I turned to the other impressive scientist: Simon Baron-Cohen, professor of developmental psychopathology and top researcher on systemizing and empathizing. Briefly, here's a paraphrase of Baron-Cohen's information:[1]

In the world we live in, two bio-neurological traits play a major role in the service of the body: they are *systemizing* and *empathizing*.

1. "The Fetal Androgen Theory of Autism." *Seaver Autism Center Newsletter* Vol. 3, #24, 2012)

Systemizing is our neurological path to activity in the inanimate world: mathematics, statistics, music, engineering, electronics, etc. It enables us to achieve systems of calculation on which we can build more elaborate systems. Take numbers, for example. Since we have ten fingers, for centuries we counted in tens and had no number zero.

Zero didn't exist until systemizers began devising mathematical schemes that enabled them to construct more complicated engineering feats. The Arabs claim they invented zero, and today we count in Arabic numbers. The Egyptians claim they invented it, and we marvel at the engineering feat it took to build the pyramids. Perhaps they both invented it. But whoever did, understood that any construction—be it a pyramid, a mathematical scheme, or an adobe hut—requires a system.

Empathizing is the neurological path to the social world. Empathy is the queasy feeling we experience when rushing a bleeding child to the emergency room—the gasp we let out when someone takes a serious fall. The word is used interchangeably with sympathy; but empathy is a feeling response, whereas sympathy is a thinking response. To put it quickly: I see a man with no legs and think "Wouldn't it be awful to have no legs!" I don't experience my thought in the same visceral, post-traumatic-stress-inducing way that a combat soldier experiences the sight of his buddy's legs being blown off.

Systemizing is a neurological trait we share intellectually. *Empathizing* is a trait we share socially and the sharing of it bonds us to one another emotionally. Once we have experienced and shared the horror of combat, we set up systems to abolish war so that others won't have to suffer the psychic pain that empathy produces.

Though empathy cannot be calibrated in the precise way that a system can, it takes both neurological traits to build a human society.

Dr. Baron-Cohen proved neurologically that men test higher than women in systemizing, and women test higher than men in empathizing.[2]

This division is not surprising; women need empathy more than men do; we bear and raise children. Baron-Cohen also devised a DVD experiment to see if he could catch this division in action. He sat a little girl in raggedy clothes (a professional child actress) on a heavily trafficked street corner. Across the street he placed a camera. Then he waited to see what would happen. Various men walked by without noticing the little girl; whether alone or with other men, they didn't give a glance. Then a woman walked by and stopped: "Dear, do you think you should be here alone?" The little girl made a semi-incoherent reply, something about how her mother said she'd be back when she was good and ready, and then began to cry. A second woman stopped, and the two women fell to wondering "What should we do? Doesn't seem right to leave the child alone. Should we call a bobby?" (the film was British) All this, caught on camera, was Baron-Cohen's way of showing us how empathy works to bind us together socially, holding us responsible for each other.

Baron-Cohen goes on to note the neurological difference in brain structure between males and females and attributes the high proportion of over-systemized autistic males to their fetal testosterone levels.[3] Though statistics vary from year to year, they tend to bear this out: there's a 3-to-1 ratio of male to female in autism; a 10-to-1 ratio in Asperger. (This doesn't mean that Aspie girls will grow a beard; it refers only to the fetal level of testosterone.)

As for the rest of us: if we're lucky, we have both systemizing and empathizing in our neurology. It makes women bold and good at math, men tender and good at creative arts. Damasio notes the value of coordinating the two traits:

2. and 3. Ibid.

"At their best, feelings point us in the proper direction, take us to the appropriate place in a decision-making space, where we may put the instruments of logic to good use."[4]

The best illustration of this was in the famous blackout of 1977, when New York City suddenly lost its electricity. With no traffic lights, cars went haywire until responsive men saw the need for a logical system. Risking danger, they strode into the middle of streets lit only by the headlights of swerving autos and began directing traffic. Drivers saw what they were doing and instantly, gratefully obeyed.

Communal life needs systems, be they the rules of a ship at sea, a country at war, or the traffic in a blacked-out city. Still, systemizing alone won't cut it. (Remember the old adage about the financial system? "Money is like blood. You need it to stay alive, but it's not what life is about.") We have to have the saving grace of empathy: that tender, untidy, personal reaction that keeps us from killing each other even when it disrupts the officially agreed upon system of a war. On Christmas Eve in the WWI trenches, there was a brief armistice between the non-commissioned men. The two sides laid down their weapons and played ball with each other.

Alas, despite our hopes for balance and good intention, history shows us that these two neurological traits tend to get at odds with each other. In one zeitgeist, systemizing can dominate; in another, empathy. The trait in command tends to tilt the cultural POV to its advantage as we once tilted slot machines to make the ball roll into the winning hole. Whichever trait reigns, there's always an unexpected price.

* * * *

4. Antonio Damasio, *Descartes' Error*, Avon Books Inc. NY 1994, intro. p. xiii

For now it's worth repeating the observable reality: autism often carries an excess of systemizing, and that can be both an amazing advantage and a severe disadvantage. The story of the mix goes something like this:

Back when the Arabs and the Egyptians added zero to mathematics, those who dreamed it up were probably Asperger. Asperger is the variety of autism often endowed with an overdose of systemizing and (as noted by Baron-Cohen) apt to be male. "Aspies" can perform mathematical magic built on logic and memory systems; they like to hold forth on their magic rather than share a conversation, and therefore have trouble making friends. Unless we help them join the world of social give-and-take they're liable to end up living in a lonely rut.

Arthur's friend Asa is an "Aspie." Asa has trouble making friends.

* * * *

As if all the obstacles I've described weren't trouble enough for Arthur and Asa and everyone else on the spectrum, there's one more obstacle that REALLY confounds them:

Social exchange has no physical reality. It's just a bunch of shared thoughts. To make it worse, each shared thought is followed by another thought—and another and another; there's no stopping the flow of ordinary social chitchat. This "unreal" state that never stops happening drives autistic kids crazy. They're frantic for the solid ground of memory and logic and physical things they can see and touch. Without it, they feel caught in an undertow that will suck them under and drown them. Hence the meltdown: a howl for help.

Though autistic meltdowns are not aimed at us personally, they feel personal. So personal and disorienting that we who are trying to help have to keep something in our pocket we can touch so we'll remember who we are.

3

THE NATURE OF OUR RESPONSE

In the years when my daughter Temple was non verbal, when she didn't want me to touch her, when she preferred to play with her spit and feces, I myself was still a child. A blank sheet of paper. I kept dreaming of empty rooms: some were beautiful with crystal chandeliers and gold wall sconces; some were spare with rough hewn wooden walls. But always they were empty. Had my undeveloped soul no furniture? No rugs, no sofa, not even a straight backed chair? How will I get to be a good mother? Or even a decent human?

One day I decided that the only way out of the emptiness would be to clean and put in order the dirtiest room in the house and work my way up, room by room, to being an acceptable member of the human race. It didn't occur to me that the task had nothing to do with understanding my child or even myself. All I could think was "Where do I start? What room do I pick?"

That's when I spotted the stairs to the cellar: "Yes! That's the room! I'll clean and put in order our old stone basement." I flipped on the wall switch, and in the dank gloom below a single light bulb dangling from a double socket let out a flicker. "Ah, a double socket. I can plug in the vacuum." I bumped the old Hoover down the cellar stairs.

"What a mess! I'll start by tidying up that heap of unwanted things too good to throw away—that'll make room to bundle the old newspapers waiting to be picked up by the Salvation Army." I nudged the newspapers with the vacuum hose; under them was a layer of dry grit that had crumbled from between the stones of the cellar wall. "OK, OK, I'll deal with that too—maybe put new cement in the wall cracks. But first the newspapers." I started to bundle the papers and an army of ants ran out. I sucked up the ants with the Hoover, but crumbs of cement grit got sucked up too and began a death rattle in the hose nozzle. I turned off the Hoover, pried the cement bits out of the hose, and laid them in a neat pile on the top cellar stair—giving the ants just enough time to send for back-up support. Out of the wall crevices came a horde of spiders. I scraped the vacuum hose over the wall and a rock dropped out. "Ahhhh! I'm not achieving redemption! I'm breaking up the foundation of our house!"

In a guilty panic I bolted up the stairs dragging the old Hoover behind me, yanking the electric cord out of the socket and blowing the dim light bulb. I wasn't even fit to clean a basement. I had no words to explain it; I didn't know I was depressed. And even if I had known, I wouldn't have admitted it. Besides, who could I admit it to?

In the early 1950s, we lived in a world where the tag end of Victorian protocol determined what we were allowed to tell each other. We wore hats and gloves, and any indication that things might not be proper at home was kept under wraps. The neighbor who didn't pay his taxes until the IRS tracked him down: did he go to jail or merely pay a fine? None of us knew; we only whispered about it. The neighbor who died of a sudden heart attack? It was years before we learned that he'd killed himself.

When the neighbors asked me what was wrong with Temple, I had to gulp to get out the words "autism" "infant schizophrenia." They asked no further; they knew what schizophrenia was. But they were staunch; they included Temple anyway. They swept my child into the neighborhood tribe and for that I am eternally grateful. It may have saved Temple's life, to say nothing of my own. But it didn't explain why I kept hiding my feelings: alarm, depression, despair, hiding them even from myself. It was years before I understood that there is no explanation for denial. Autism is overwhelming, and we hide. Mothers admit their feelings only to close friends, show them occasionally in overweight. We hunger for love from a baby whose autism causes such social isolation that we cannot even enjoy the homely game of peek-a-boo. A baby needs a mother to know she's a baby, but a mother needs a baby to know she's a mother.

And dads?

At a recent conference, a strapping Texas dad, six feet tall and 200 pounds, struggles to tell me about his half grown son and burst into tears. He's so overwhelmed by his boy that he no longer feels he's the honorable man he thought he was. Stammering incoherently, he begs me to give him a hug. We hug and in that strained moment, he becomes—what? A shame-filled child asking for forgiveness? A self-absorbed adolescent who wants out? My guess is the hug is an SOS. He aches to leave his family so he can reclaim his honor, but he knows the unjust toll it will take. He may jump ship anyway, but if he does, he will leave damaged.

Siblings, too, will be damaged. It's not just that they're reduced to being little helpers—and that happens—they're deprived of a sense of their own emotional growth, and they're too young to understand what they're losing. An autistic child is praised extravagantly for achieving or even approximating behavior that's expected from siblings, but no one praises the sibling. At school games autistic kids can be bad sports; they equate game-winning with the praise they get for good behavior. So when they follow the game rules and don't win, they're furious and vent. The sibling stands by, silent and mortified, while his little friends snicker. He can't speak up for fear he'll look disloyal. Nobody praises him for his loyalty, or even notices it.

Meanwhile the autistic kid has discovered that tantrums get him what he wants. Since the sibling hasn't lived long enough to understand the unfair advantage of this, he accepts the role of "smoothing the path" without understanding its cost. It may soon become his identity.

Stress compounds when families take an autistic kid into a store or restaurant. Despite an educated press, the everyday world disapproves of public meltdowns, and when it happens, they're apt to tell off parents. Then when parents explain, remorse sets in, and they suffer the nagging feeling that they've not been the kindly folk they thought they were. There's no getting around it: we're socially connected creatures, incomplete without each other.

In 1624 the poet John Donne told us: "No man is an island, entire of itself. Every man is a piece of the continent." Four hundred years later, bio-neurologist V.S. Ramachandran affirmed Donne's words in scientific terms:

> "... the uniquely human sense of self is not an 'airy nothing' without habitation and a name... the self actually emerges from a reciprocity of interacts with others..."[1]

Where there's autism, reciprocity doesn't always work.

At a recent autism conference, I told a version of all this and included the tale of cleaning my basement. During the break a mother introduced me to her seven-year-old autistic son. "He'd like to ask you a question."

"Why did you want to clean that old basement?" he asked. "It doesn't make sense."

1. *The Tell-Tale Brain*, Norton & Co. 2011.

"No, it doesn't, but that's what I did."

"Why?"

"I don't know why."

The boy kept on asking. He wanted to know logically why I, the autism expert, would do such a dumb thing. If he could learn why—maybe learn straight from the horse's mouth—then he wouldn't be so thrown off by other people's dumb behavior.

"Tell me the story again."

"I can't."

"Why not?"

"We've used up all the break time."

The boy accepted that answer. He'd learned in school that when the bell rings, time's up, class is over; that's the rule. He saw the conference break as being like school. So "time's up" —to his way of thinking—was a logical, rule-based answer to a logical question.

For me, hiding my feelings from my conscious self by vacuuming the cellar was a temporary solution to the stress of autism. At the same time, dreams of empty rooms were signaling an existential quandary I had yet to deal with. How could I explain that to a child? Besides, the boy didn't want a "feeling" answer; he wanted a logical answer.

I thought of Arthur, the boy in the second chapter. He, too, wanted a logical world. His delight in *Jeopardy* wasn't just in the questions and answers, but that logic and memory didn't stir up feelings in him that he couldn't deal with. Also, he'd found in the program a camaraderie. Though the contestants were in competition, they seemed to like each other and enjoy each other's command of facts. Sometimes Arthur knew the *Jeopardy* answer before they did, and it made him feel connected to the group. Information is most fun when there's somebody to tell it to.

Unwittingly—Arthur, the questioning boy, and I—were each of us in our own way trying to deal with psychic loneliness. Arthur by joining forces with information, the questioning boy by investing in logic, and I by thinking I could clean and tidy up what the poet Yeats called *"the foul rag and bone shop of the human heart."*

Yeats dreamed up those words in 1937, when WWII was about to burst into flames. We were all too frightened then (and too busy gunning up) to stop and wonder how in our forgotten pre-history, we had emerged from instinct driven herd animals marking our territory with urine into "self" aware, "idea" aware, death aware humans.

Twenty-three years earlier, in 1914, hikers had fallen through a gap in the rocky underbrush of southwest France. The gap had led to passages, the passages to underground chambers, and the chambers held what looked to be ancient ceremonial symbols.

4

MAN, THE DREAMER

Part One

"He was becoming something the world had never seen before—a dream animal—living at least partially within a secret universe of his own creation and sharing that secret universe in his head with other, similar heads. Symbolic communication had begun. Man had escaped out of the eternal present of the animal world into a knowledge of past and future. The unseen gods, the powers behind the world of phenomenal appearance, began to stalk through his dream."[1]

It's odd to think of speech as "symbolic communication." But when you break down the steps those long-ago dream animals had to go through in order to share their secret universe with each other, it turns out that "words" are highly motivated, cooperative, and—yes—symbolic. Somehow or other, in the long stretches of forgotten time, we humans developed the knack of turning our animal yelps into individual vocals, each vocal standing for (symbolizing) an object, a creature, or an action.

1. Loren Eiseley: The Immense Journey, Vintage, 1946, '50, '53 © Eiseley, '56, '57

Alert signals among the animals must have already existed. (Witness the jays in my garden hollering at the sparrows when the cat was on the prowl.) The symbolic human version probably developed first as a means of survival in the tooth-and-claw battle with beasts more wily and powerful than us. But it only worked if we understood it together as a tribe—and individually. Each human had to get the gist of it on his own. Speech was—and still is—a learned process.

Nevertheless, one way or another, we achieved it—

"... long before previously thought, in some cases more than 40,000 years...We have sufficient evidence to the effect that Neanderthals possessed a symbolic culture."[2]

In the Spanish cave called El Castillo, prehistorians have found groups of handprints made by each tribe member putting a hand on the cave wall and blowing red ochre around it. Similar handprints have been found in caves far distant from each other—sometimes those of men, women, and children.

Depositphotos

2. (Dr. Joao Zilao, prehistorian at the University of Barcelona *The New York Times: Science* 6/15/2012)

How did tribes living at vast distances from each other come to share the same ceremony? And how many years did it take? When prehistorians refer to 40,000 years ago, we forget how long that time stretch is.

* * * *

Thirty thousand years ago (10,000 years after Spanish El Castillo) men holding flaming torches crawled deep into a gorge of the river Ardeche in Southern France and, with charcoal from earlier fires, drew on its walls their vision of animals: lions, horses, reindeer and rhino. For the first time animal drawings appear. France has other caves with similar drawings, some dating 17,000 years later. Some (like the cave mentioned in Chapter 3) reachable only by mile-long crawls through limestone passages—hazardous journeys to caverns where a more advanced shaman magic honored the uncanny power that ruled both animals and humans. Ancient bone flutes have also been found—flutes that a musician can blow a tune on. Did the tunes imitate the cries of wounded animals, the yells of hunters, the grieving moans of mother animals whose young had been slaughtered? Or crickets, bird calls, and the whine of cicadas? Was it to appease a power greater than humans or to delight humans? Or both? Were we—together with the animals—filled with wonder and awe; and a need to express it?

The question reminds me today of a magnificent sunset on Martha's Vineyard. As a group of us watched the sun drop into the Vineyard Sound, throwing its dazzling glow over the inlet and across the beach grass, we realized two cottontail rabbits were also watching, sitting bolt upright on their hunkers, their paws held like begging dogs. If we'd made a move, they would have scampered, but for a moment they—and us—were transfixed.

How did we dream up the imitative magic that would transform us into worshipping humans? And who would rule the magic? Not impossible to imagine. Over and over a man has recorded another, more telling kind of handprint on the wall of the Ardeche cave: a hand with a crooked little finger. Are the drawings his, and has the tribe (or maybe other shamans?) allowed him his handprint— perhaps even celebrated it? The crooked little finger turns up in other caves.

Tribes must have crawled their way through those cave passages carrying torches—a feat that required hands with opposable thumbs. Though apes have hands that look like ours, their thumbs do not work in opposition to the fingers; and that limits their ability to manipulate sizable objects. Only with the help of an opposable thumb could men have crawled through narrow cave passages carrying lighted torches.

Opposable thumbs also enabled them to draw.

Limestone caves have stalactites and stalagmites. When shamans aimed their flaming torches at them and found themselves spattered with sparkling prisms of color, they must have felt transformed. Such an effect would turn any human into an awed, self-aware self in the company of other selves—all of them in the presence of an unseen force greater than they were. A symbol of that force deserved to be recorded on every cave wall.

Then somehow, in the welter of lost eons, the symbol grew to be more than an external representation. Symbolic thinking became a permanent feature of our genetic neurology. As far as we know, humans are the only animals that think symbolically.

With the exception of those with autism.

* * * *

Today a doctor can check a child's ability to think symbolically by using the old game of "make-believe," a scheme invented by Catherine Lord, renowned autism authority, Dr. Lord picks up a toy block, waves it through the air, and makes a humming sound. "Hummmmm. I'm a plane," she says. Most children are likely to respond by picking up another block, pushing it around the floor, and saying, "Broooom! I'm a truck." Each child has turned the block into a symbol that stands for another object and made the sound that stands for the sound of that object. (Erik Erikson, Developmental Psychologist, has noted that the way children play with toys indicates the way they will play with thoughts.) Many children also draw symbolically. They draw a square, put a triangle on top of it, and say, "That's my house." They draw a stick figure with a circle for a head, put two little circles in the head for eyes, and say, "That's Daddy." Then they draw a littler stick figure with a littler head and say, "That's Mommy." Children accept each other's make-believe. Not so autism. Give an autistic child a bunch of toy blocks, and chances are he will line them up. The symbolic element of make-believe escapes him. When everyday life with all its confusing detail comes rushing at him, it's no wonder he lines up his toy blocks. He's trying to set up a meaningful system with which to deal with life's daily chaos.

Now think of a boy like Arthur in Chapter Two living in the era of Ardeche. The frightening impact of a powerful shaman leading a tribal ritual. It doesn't take much to imagine shamans with red ochre decorating their faces, the tribe dancing around them chanting and drumming with animal bones on skins stretched over hollow tree stumps—the shamans holding aloft glittering stalactites they've hacked from the limestone caves, waving them in the firelight, making them spatter rainbow magic on a frenzied tribe that's working itself up to an orgasmic ecstasy.

What if Arthur—terrified by the din, the chaos—a painted shaman, his "god" face grinning at him in the firelight—had gone into shrieking hysterics: the first autistic meltdown?

Would the tribe have accepted him? Or would they have abandoned him in the forest to be killed and devoured by a pack of wolves? When did intolerance enter our dreams? Or was it always there—a herd instinct we clung to as we spiraled upwards, dizzy with release from the old animal laws?

Part Two
Trapped Souls

After we dreamed up symbolic thinking and used it to empower us over the other animals, we dreamed up how we thought the world *ought* to be. And the children who could not behave as we thought they ought to behave, we called "changelings." In the centuries of recorded history when witchcraft was alive and well, we said that children like Arthur were the bewitched offspring of nature spirits. When you run across the instructions for ridding a town of changelings, you wonder how we could have thought up and carried out anything so cruel and so crazy.

But we did.

Consider the detail in the following picture. It's taken from a 1559 painting by Pieter Bruegel the Elder, entitled *Netherlandish Proverbs*. The painting hangs in the Staatliche Museum, Berlin.

Art book authorities tell us that each cluster of characters in this painting crowded with people illustrates a proverb, but they admit they're at a loss to explain the proverb illustrated in the lower left-hand corner where a disturbing task is underway. A child is being tied up; he could be autistic or he could have fetal alcohol syndrome. Either way, it's quite possible he's been pronounced a *changeling* and is being prepared for a ritual burning. If so, the preparations don't seem to bother any of the surrounding characters, save for a nearby boy who clings to a log of wood. Art authorities tell us the boy is a symbol of hypocrisy, but it could be that he fears he's about to be the next. Bruegel had a sly way of depicting the appalling as ordinary.

Here's the gist of the folk tale instructions:

"Before a mortal baby is christened, don't let him wear green ribbons. For the faeries will see the green, steal him away and put one of their own in its place. It will look like your child, but instead of speaking, it will croak and hum and take revenge on you with obscene tricks. A

changeling child has no Christian soul. You must throw it on the fire. The flames will strip it of its enchanted shape, so it will have no choice but to fly back to its faery home."

These ancient instructions are so collectively damning that—as bio-neurologist Eric Kandel suggests—tribal rejection could be in our neurology:

"...future research on the factors that enable members of a cohesive group to recognize one another, may also teach us something about the factors that give rise to tribalism, which is so often associated with fear, hatred, and intolerance of outsiders."[3]

Dr. Kandel opened his 2007 lecture at the New York 92nd Street YMHA with a recollection of his painful childhood as a Viennese Jew suffering under the brutal tribalism of the Nazis. For Kandel to suggest that such behavior might be neurological is generous in the extreme, and from the look of early folklore, he could be right. Long before the Nazis, tribal intolerance had already lodged itself in our timeworn fairy tales in the shape of giants, ogres, elves, witches, and trolls—physical grotesqueries that even today strike fear and hatred in our childish hearts. That ancient reaction may well have included fear of odd children who avoided human contact and wouldn't speak. Given their lack of social response they too, could have been judged the eerie offspring of those pre-Christian nature spirits: the faeries.
According to Wikipedia:

"Belief in changelings lasted in parts of Ireland until 1895 when Bridget Cleary was killed by her husband who believed her to be a changeling."

3. *In Search of Memory.* Norton 2006

For some Irish the belief is still alive. At a recent autism conference, a mother brought me a turn-of-the-century photograph of her grandfather, taken when he was a little boy with long curls. The curls, she said, were to fool the faeries into thinking he was a girl because faeries prefer male children. (Autism tends to be 3-to-1 male) The mother told me that when she was a baby and was slow learning to talk, her mother believed she was a changeling. I asked her if she was Irish. She said "Of course."

Another historic way of dealing with infants declared "not human" was to abandon them in lonely woods: live bait for wild animals. From this practice sprang tales to comfort grieving mothers, each mother praying that her baby would be found and suckled by a forgiving beast.

The Roman statue of the mother wolf standing guard over the twins, Romulus and Remus—her milk dripping into their open mouths—would be recreated in each era as the yearning for comfort stories increased with the practice of abandonment.

Literary versions of this folk tale were to turn up in the late nineteenth and early twentieth centuries—stories like Kipling's tale of Mowgli, a boy raised by the wild animals of India (1893) and Burroughs' novel of Tarzan raised by the African apes (1912). Both boys have an eerie strangeness to them, but interpretation of their strangeness has shifted. Under the spell of nineteenth-century romanticism, Mowgli and Tarzan are deemed "pure": unencumbered with worldly knowledge and incapable of lies. "Eerie" and "pure" are two sides of the same coin.

By far the most touching of these stories isn't literary at all. It's the nineteenth-century account of Victor, the "Wild Boy of Aveyron," recorded in the notebook of a young French medical intern: Jean-Marc Gaspard Itard. In 1969, French filmmaker Francois Truffaut, working from Itard's notebook and playing the part of Dr. Itard himself, produced a film about Victor called *The Wild Child*. I doubt if Truffaut realized Victor was autistic. It would take another twenty years for autism authority Uta Frith, also working from Itard's notebook, to observe that all signs of Victor's behavior would "...*be familiar to the parent of a child with typical autism today despite the time difference of nearly two centuries.*"[4]

Today Victor has made it into Wikipedia, where he's described as emerging around 1808 from the dense woods of Southern France: a ten-year-old, bushy-haired kid wearing nothing but a tattered shirt. According to Wikipedia, his food preferences and the numerous scars on his body indicated he'd lived in the wild the majority of his life.

Had he? If so, why was he wearing a tattered shirt? How come he knew how to dig potatoes and boil beans? Dr. Itard writes in his notebook about the thick scar on Victor's throat—a scar that appears to be about three years old—but he doesn't speculate as to its cause. Perhaps because it looked too much like the work of changeling believers.

Had Victor's mother, knowing Victor could survive on his own in the wild, let her boy hide in the woods in order to keep

4. *Autism Explaining the Enigma*. Oxford: Basil Blackwell. 1989

him safe from changeling captors? I think of a twentieth century father in Utah who told me that his severely autistic son would be perfectly capable of surviving by himself in the wooded mountains of Utah.

Or was running away an old habit of Victor's? Autistic boys are known to be "bolters," running away because they feel like it, because they've been asked to do something they don't want to do, and, in Victor's case, running away to survive. Victor was non verbal; he had no way to tell his mother who was the man who'd tried to cut his throat. Was the man alone or were there other men with him—all of them of them shrieking "Devil's child?" Did the boy slimy with blood slip from their grasp and flee into the woods? A piece of the story is missing: questions that Itard, in 1808, may have been afraid to ask, and Truffaut could only hint at. (In Truffaut's film, a gang of men with ratting terriers capture Victor.)

Itard's notebook tells of a local abbot who was also a professor of biology. It's possible that the abbot stopped the men from killing the boy. He, too, figured Victor to be about ten, and he, too, dated the knife scar as three years old. Wanting to know how much cold the boy could withstand; he had taken Victor into the snowy woods and undressed him. Far from being cold, Victor frolicked about in the nude. The abbot then concluded that the human reaction to temperature was due to "conditioning and experience."[5]

Had he also concluded that Victor was not a changeling, but just an odd little boy? Did he write Dr. Philippe Pinel of the Paris Salpêtrière Hospital asking for a medical authority to come and rescue the child? And did Dr. Pinel send his young medical intern, Itard? All of this is possible. There's a scene in Truffaut's film where Itard and Dr. Pinel consult together over Victor, who, for the first time, is seeing himself in a mirror.

5. Wikipedia

Alamy

Dr. Pinel was known internationally for his advanced and humane treatment of the insane. Check the internet for his name, and up will come the famous painting of his releasing the insane from bondage.

When Itard brought Victor to Pinel, the two doctors must have been aware that they would have to deal with the political "bed of hot coals" going on between Enlightenment and the Church. In that time slot, there were shouted arguments on every Paris street corner—all quite different from Aveyron where most of the time the Abbot's authority ruled. In Aveyron, so hearsay has it, Victor was known to turn up at kitchen doors, ragged and hungry. Mothers fed him and never told. Silence was their way of dealing with the changeling superstition.

Nevertheless the belief was everywhere. Twenty years after Victor, a teenager named Kasper Hauser turned up on the streets of Nuremburg Germany claiming he'd been raised alone in a darkened cell. Today Nuremberg honors him with a statue, but his history and behavior suggest autism and tribal rejection. Five years after turning up, Kasper was stabbed to death.

Tribal rejection is with us still. A few years ago, I met a female version of Victor. Now middle-aged, she told me how as a young girl her parents had declared her "not human," and on a lonely road through a stretch of forest, threw her out of the car to fend for herself. Still hardly grown, maybe as old as twelve, she survived for two years living off what she scavenged in the way of nuts and berries, and what she could kill. She had a shotgun she'd bought at a rifle store. Despite being underage with no I.D. and an odd way of speaking, she'd saved a little money and the store was happy to take it. She shot small woodland animals: rabbits and squirrels and sometimes fawns. She knew how to make a fire by rubbing two sticks together; she could skin and cook the meat over the fire and eat it for days until "it tasted funny." (Somehow she escaped food poisoning.)

It wasn't the meat that upset her; it was the fawns she shot for their meat. As she saw the light dim in their almost human eyes—and faced the physical fact they were dying so that she could live—she accepted death in a way that Arthur may never. As she told me her tale, I wondered if she understood that she herself would one day die. All I know is that after two years in the woods she managed somehow to find her way to becoming a surprisingly successful jockey. "I never used a whip," she said. "The horse and I, we both wanted to win. So we just talked to each other."

Today her family wants her back. They've gotten wind of her jockey skill and now see her as a money maker. Because she's autistic, they know they can claim legal custody. So she lives in hiding, secretly protected by the two women who brought her to me. Unlike Victor's story which Itard recorded in his notebook; this woman's tale lives only in hearsay. I promised the two who are protecting her that I wouldn't reveal her whereabouts. But her face lives with me always.

Despite middle age, it's the face of a child.

5

THE BED OF HOT COALS

The bed of hot coals waiting in Paris for Itard and Victor was the war between Enlightenment and the church. Itard's notebook doesn't detail the fiery arguments going on between "Natural Philosophy" and ecclesiastical authority, nor does it touch on the church crusade against witchcraft.

Witchcraft

Long ago, when speech gave us the edge over the other animals, we looked for ways to interpret the success or failure of our journey through life. We interpreted disaster as punishment, but we had no way to explain good luck. Eerie coincidences kept happening—sometimes to our un-earned advantage.

According to generations of the faithful, witchcraft was the *manipulation* of spirit forces in order to gain control over another person or situation. Prayer, on the other hand, was a *supplication* to a higher spirit in hope of forgiveness for a regretted act. Both acts sought control; both acts believed in the power of the other. Two spirit beings: God and the Devil.

Though we have no reliable knowledge of past belief patterns, it doesn't take much to interpret an epileptic seizure as a state of religious or demonic ecstasy depending on which power you believe in. As late as 1947, the prayer book rite of exorcism, a religious ceremony to drive forth the demonic power possessing someone, informs the priest in Instruction #19:

"...Always have responsible people, preferably relatives, to hold down the woman while the devil is agitating her."

For anyone familiar with autism, that instruction could also be advice for handling an epileptic seizure (epilepsy and autism are linked) or for the restraint needed during a violent autistic meltdown. Though autism is predominately male, the prayer book reads "the woman."

From 1450 to 1750, church-endorsed witch hunts were underway in Europe. By 1484 Cologne had published the punitive *Malleus Maleficarum*, known as the "Hammer of Witches. The *Malleus* explained in detail how to recognize a witch (usually a woman) and what punishments to deliver. In opposition to belief in witchcraft was the growing knowledge of nature and of medicine. Educated studies of both were beginning to give voice to a new understanding of the phenomenal world—a voice that in time would coalesce into the Enlightenment. The first signs of this new thinking arrived as early as 1584 (100 years after the *Malleus*) when Reginald Scott, an Oxford educated Englishman committed to fighting superstition, wrote *The Discoverie of Witchcraft*.[1] His aim was to end the persecution of witches, many of whom, he noted, were merely old and poor and a little demented. Scott was also intent on exposing charlatans who were profiting from belief in sorcery.

1. Oxford Companion to English Lit., Oxford Univ. Press 1944

Nevertheless, belief in witchcraft persisted and crossed the Atlantic to turn up in New England 100 years later. In Salem Massachusetts in 1692, nineteen women were hanged for witchcraft, fifty-five were frightened into confessions, 150 were imprisoned, and a man named Giles Corey was pressed to death with rocks. In time the Salem accusers (learned, patrician men) regretted their act and recanted, but it was a bit late. Witchcraft trials continued to prevail. Germany's 1735 Witchcraft Act still pronounced sorcery punishable by law; Britain continued its trials until the close of the eighteenth century. None of it ended the belief and practice of witchcraft. Village sorcery simply joined forces with rites ordained by the church. Both were magic. Both must be obeyed.

I doubt if Itard believed in sorcery, nor would the abbot. Itard was a doctor, and the abbot a biologist. But both men were Catholics, and the Church declared the words of the Holy Bible to be God incarnate:

"In the beginning was the Word, and the Word was with God, and the Word was God."[2]

Ergo, the Church said, anyone who was deaf from birth and couldn't speak the word of God was "not fully human."[3]

Though Itard knew Victor wasn't deaf, he realized that teaching him to speak would be the only way to prove to the church and the superstitious that he was not the "changeling" child of witchcraft but a real little boy with an immortal soul. Nevertheless, undertaking the task would walk the two of them through a religious and political bed of hot coals.

2. The Holy Bible *Authorized King James Version* John 1:1-3
3. Jerome Groopman *NYRB* article Dec 7, 2017

Enlightenment

Had the nineteenth-century Church not noticed how Enlightenment thinking had been working its disguised way into Christian art? That, over the spread of years, paintings of sacred scenes were being covertly rearranged into celebrations of *Natural Philosophy*? It had started in the seventeenth century and been slyly slipping into view without causing any alarm among the faithful or even awareness of what the rearrangements implied.

In 1632 Rembrandt painted his *Anatomy Lesson of Dr. Tulp*. For another 200 years, dissection of dead human bodies would be considered a sin, yet here was a painting of a cadaver being cut open by a well known physician, and it's lit like the *Descent from the Cross*. Clustered around the cadaver—where once Apostles gathered—a group of doctors leans in to learn.

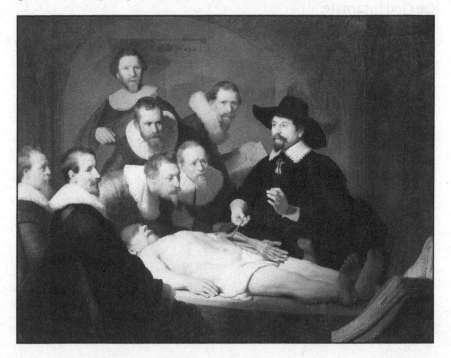

A hundred years later, Enlightenment had crept in further. In 1768 Wright of Derby painted his *Experiment with an Air Pump*. The air pump is lit like a haloed crèche. Instead of worshipping shepherds and Wise Men, a group of knowledge seekers are gathered around it; and where once an angel hovered overhead a demonstrator stands.

Yes, the church had noticed, and it was cause for worry. Thus far interpretation of life's meaning had come under the Papal voice, one that preached the faith of Saint Thomas Aquinas and Saint Augustine. Now the church was losing ground to secular thinkers; men proclaiming the authority of Sir Isaac Newton who had put forth his laws of motion and his idea of universal gravitation (1682). Even more alarming, David Hume, in his 1752 *Treatise of Human Nature*, had written that the evidence for miracles was necessarily inferior to evidence for the laws of nature. These men were calling their blasphemy "Natural Philosophy."

Dr. Itard was in a further bind. In the church interpretation of "soul," early nineteenth-century philosophers looked to the work of seventeenth-century mathematician/philosopher Rene Descartes. Descartes had proclaimed that: (a) "the control of animal inclination by thought, reason, and the will was what made us human—and (b) thinking was "an activity quite separate from the body," ergo the property of God. * The (b) part was where Victor presented a problem. Because he showed no sign of reason, thought, or will, where could his "soul" (if he had one) reside?[4]

Since Victor was non verbal, Itard housed him first in an institution for the deaf and dumb. When he realized he wasn't deaf, he took him into his own home. It was there that he struggled to teach Victor to speak—working by rote, canning him when he thought it necessary and leashing him when they went out walking (most likely the way Itard himself had been taught). And if Victor tended to bolt (as Itard soon discovered), what was there for it but a leash? Alas, the only word Victor could ever speak was "lait," the French word for milk.

Did any of it matter? All Victor understood was that he could no longer scramble up walnut trees in the wooded countryside of Aveyron or feel the warmth of his mother's arms. As he reached adolescence, Itard tried to teach him the proper behavior with women by introducing him to a young girl. Victor hadn't a clue what that was about. Yet when Itard learned that Victor had seen the housekeeper weeping and tried to console her, he figured he had finally taught Victor how to empathize and cherish. Had he? Or had the housekeeper and Victor's mother loved Victor just as he was, and Victor loved them in return? Two simple country women whose devotion to the boy and belief in God did not spring from intellectual Paris arguments but from warm hearts. Victor

4. *Descartes' Error: Emotion, Reason, and the Human Brain* Antonio Damasio, Avon Books Inc. NYC 1995)

died at twenty-eight, but for those two women he would always be twelve years old frolicking nude in the woods of Aveyron, released into a moment of pure animal joy.

Systemizing and Empathizing in Conflict

Early nineteenth-century philosophy and natural philosophy sheltered a mix of disciplines. David Hume was also an historian, economist, and essayist; Isaac Newton was a theologian and alchemist. Brilliant minds didn't limit their thinking or their friendship to a single focus. Now a new, highly systemized discipline was about to take over.

In 1833, William Whewell would invent the word "science" from the Latin word *scientia*, meaning knowledge. His intention was to assert and formulate a body of work based solely on provable formulae that would hold true for all time. Though Whewell and his "New Scientists" hadn't entirely forsaken belief in God, they looked darkly on the unprovable complexities of empathy.

In contrast to the New Scientists were the writers and poets. Calling themselves "Romantics," they were already celebrating their un-provable empathy in words that school children would learn by heart:

> *For oft when on my couch I lie in vacant or in pensive mood*
> *They flash upon that inward eye which is the bliss of solitude:*
> *And then my heart with pleasure fills*
> *And dances with the daffodils.* [5]

In fairness to Whewell and his New Scientists, the battle between the two behavior styles may not have been entirely due to the bio-neurological difference between systemizing and

5. William Wordsworth: "I Wandered Lonely as a Cloud," 1802

empathizing, but to the social upbringing of nineteenth-century males. As schoolboys, the New Scientists would have been taught to repress emotion and fight for their country (a perfect mindset for conquering and dominating foreign territories). Accustomed to a constrained obedience, they were ready to commit to New Science without questioning it.

"Define and categorize the phenomenal world," they were told, "and back up your findings with statistically provable experiments."

Though valuable, the procedure not only side stepped empathy, but left unexplored the nature of the phenomenon (concept) and *why* it was happening. In some inarticulate way, the Romantics were thinking both conceptually and emotionally but had no way to prove their point of view. They could only tell stories, catalogue the stories, and call the result "mysticism." I looked up "mysticism" in Webster's and found that even old Noah had trouble defining it. I'm not surprised; there's something uncanny about thinking conceptually and something ludicrous about empathy. You cut your finger, and because of empathy, I say "ouch." It defies good sense. Why would I feel faint at the sight of your bleeding finger? On the other hand, there's something logical, reliable, and highly respectable ("respectable" mattered to Victorians) about systemizing phenomenal reality. Since the New Scientists were raised not to question authority, giving in to an un-systemized emotion must have struck them as heresy. Their reaction? "Suppress it." Or at best call it, a "soft science." Something women do. And what respectable Victorian gentleman would want to think like a woman?

In a literary search to verify what I suspected the Romantics were muttering angrily behind closed doors, I ran into a quote from Edgar Allan Poe (1809–1840), who called the New Scientists "diggers and peddlers of minute facts" who belong in the "sculleries" of the mind rather than the "parlors." Their methodical reasoning, he sneered: "creeps and crawls and blinds itself with the Scotch snuff of detail." At that particular time, Poe was writing mystery stories starring C. Auguste Dupin, the French detective who identified "his intellect with that of another...thereby divining what that person must think or do. He called Dupin's way of thinking "the fusing power of poetic imagination."[6] Today we call it empathy.

Nevertheless, in his battle with the New Scientists, Poe seems to have been unable (or unwilling) to fuse his own poetic imagination with "methodical reason." One way or another, the Romantics and the New Scientists were not going to like each other.

AN ODD PAIR.

"ONE SHOE OFF, AND ONE SHOE ON,
DIDDLE-DIDDLE-DUMPKIN, NORTHAMP-TON."—*Nursery Rhyme.*

6. *Major Writers of America*, Harcourt Brace, 1962

AUTISM IN VICTORIAN LITERATURE

In 1798, William Wordsworth wrote "The Idiot Boy," a ballad about a boy "not as wise as some folks be." Composed in folk song style, it tells of old Betty Foy, the boy's mother: her frantic concern for Johnny, his whereabouts and safety. She's sent him on his pony to summon help for an ill neighbor, and he's wandered off—God knows where.

The highpoint of the ballad is Johnny himself. When old Betty finally finds him, he's still astride his pony but has forgotten the ill neighbor. Instead he's glorying in the night, happy to recount to his mother how:

"*The cocks did crow to whoo, to whoo,*
And the sun did shine so cold."

He thinks the owls are roosters and the full moon is the sun. Meanwhile, Wordsworth tells us, the ill neighbor has recovered miraculously on her own. The ballad reads like the kind of yarn country folk would spin, but Wordsworth's fans saw no value in a tale about a lad they believed was "half witted." (They may also have believed Johnny's addled glory in the moon and the owls was proof he was a changeling.) Wordsworth defended his ballad and said it was about mother love, no less valuable for being unreasonable.

In the same cultural span as Wordsworth's ballad, young Dr. Itard in France had taken on the role of parenting Victor. Though he had a housekeeper, she couldn't manage the boy without his help. While Itard was assisting her, he was also trying to teach Victor to speak —an impossible task given Victor's autism. Had unreasonable love taken hold of Itard as it had of Wordsworth's Old Betty? Were both poet and doctor struggling to come to terms with the gap between reason and passion?

Alamy

Note the change in attitude from the earlier picture of Itard and Pinel examining Victor.

Again I searched for clues, and this time I found Wordsworth's prose argument on the value of poetry (passion) vs. that of science (reason). Ever the literary gentleman, Wordsworth appears to be groping for a way to honor science while holding tight his belief in the superior power of poetry:

"The man of science seeks truth as a remote and unknown benefactor; he cherishes and loves it in his solitude; the poet, singing a song in which all human beings join with him, rejoices in the presence of truth as our visible friend and hourly companion..."

"...Emphatically may it be said of the poet, as Shakespeare hath said of man, that he "looks before and after." He is the rock of defense for human nature... carrying everywhere with him relationship and love..."[1]

There in stilted nineteenth-century epistle style is the same old battle, this time composed by a much more generous hearted poet than Edgar Allan Poe.

****

Charles Dickens was an extrovert; no "wandering lonely as a cloud" for him! He began his writing career as a reporter and journalist covering London's social life. His first novel, *The Pickwick Papers* (1837), detailed the comic misadventures of the Pickwick Club and took no note of social injustice. A year later, now ready to commit to just that, Dickens wrote *Nicholas Nickleby*. The novel revolves around Smike, a lad not too different from Wordsworth's "Idiot Boy," but instead of being accepted and loved, he has been hidden in a disreputable school for "repudiated" boys (Dickens' word). Known as Dotheboys Hall, the school is run by the one-eyed Wackford Squeers, who brutally maltreats forty urchins under the pretense of education.

Unaware of any of this, our hero, Nicholas Nickleby, takes a teaching job at Dotheboys Hall where he finds Smike, the timid, dull-witted son of his rich Uncle Ralph. Wakeford Squeers has reduced Smike to an unhappy drudge. In the original "Phiz"

1. *Norton Anthology of English Literature*, Vol 2, W.W. Norton & Co. NY, 1962

illustrations, Smike is drawn as a skinny, disheveled wreck, almost as tall as Nicholas but beardless. Whether he is autistic or developmentally slow or just plain abused, it's never fully clear, but his responses to Nicholas read like autism. All Dickens tells us is that Smike is older than the other boys and has been banished to Dotheboys Hall for life.

Though there were rumors of such schools, Victorian readers refused to believe them. Indignant, they wrote Dickens: "This is an outrage! No such schools exist in Yorkshire!"

"Yes, they do," crowed Dickens, and proceeded to publish how he had learned of them.

"*... these Yorkshire school masters were the lowest and most rotten round in the whole ladder. Traders in the avarice, indifference, or imbecility of parents, and the helplessness of children: ignorant, sordid, brutal men to whom few considerate personas would have entrusted the board or lodging of a horse or a dog...*

...they formed the worthy cornerstone of a structure, which, for absurdity and a magnificent high-minded laissez-aller neglect, has rarely been exceeded in the world..."

Ever the reporter, Dickens couldn't resist publishing his full report:

"...*I went down into Yorkshire before I began this book...I wanted to see a school master or two, and was forewarned that those gentlemen might, in their modesty, be shy of receiving a visit from the author of* The Pickwick Papers."

Given the nineteenth-century "corduroy" roads (logs laid down to get a horse and coach through swampy stretches), Dickens' trip to Yorkshire must have been a rough one. When the horse couldn't pull the coach through the muck, everyone had to get out to lighten the load. All the male passengers (Dickens included) would have then put their backs to the coach and heaved it free—while the driver coaxed the horse forward.

When Dickens finally reached a Yorkshire Inn, he would have had to inveigle a local to meet him for an informative dinner. No doubt the innkeeper knew Dickens was a celebrity, but would a local know? Yes, of course. Gossip travels fast in a small village—which was probably why a local agreed to talk to Dickens only at an inn and not his home. He wouldn't have wanted his wife with her ear to the parlor door.

The evening arrives. The innkeeper piles fresh logs on the fire, pulls a table up close, and sets out his best port. Dickens, cleaned up (a bucket of hot water would have been delivered to his room) descends the stair and greets the local. The local gives a stiff bow and touches his cap. The two sit down. Dickens uncorks the port with his pocketknife, pours them each a glass, and raises his in a toast. The innkeeper's wife serves them her best meal, and the local tells her it's better than his wife's. All goes swimmingly; no doubt the local is flattered to be dining with a celebrity. Yet, after two hours of food and wine, he's confided no information. Not to be outdone, Dickens writes that he fabricated what he calls "a pious fraud." He tells the local he's helping a widow find a school for her son, but every time he says the word "school," the conversation stalls. Dickens persists; he hasn't traveled all this way not to get his story. The local sighs. It's time to come clean:

> "Weel Misther... ar'll spak my moind tiv'ee. Dinnot let the weedur send her lattle boy to yan o' our school-measthers... ar wouln't mak' ill words amang my neeburs, and ar tiv'ee quiet loike. But I'm dom'd if ar can gang to bed and not tellee, for weedur's sak, to keep the lattle boy from a' sike scoondrels..."[2]

That's how Dickens learned about the Yorkshire schools and passed the news on to his readers: "...Mr. Squeers and his school are faint and feeble pictures of an existing reality..."[3]

Literary critics interpret Smike as the shadow self of Nicholas, whom they interpret as the shadow self of Dickens. When Dickens was ten years old, he was put to work in a shoe blacking warehouse

2., 3., and 4. *Nicholas Nickleby* 1839

pasting labels on boot blacking bottles, most likely in the company of "boys of stunted growth... the bleared eye, the harelip, the crooked foot."[4]

Though now a popular author, known and fêted in Britain and the States, he never forgot what it felt like to be *repudiated*.

* * * *

In Dickens's later novel *Our Mutual Friend*, the storyteller in him takes over from the journalist, and he gives us two cherished autistics: Jennie Wren, the doll's dressmaker, and "Sloppy," her

incipient suitor. Though innocent of full intelligence, Sloppy can read the newspaper—a boon to Victorian illiterates. Jennie Wren, with her old-lady-maiden-aunt way, is undersized, crippled, and distinctly odd, yet she's found her way to a small career making outfits for dolls. She succeeds because of kindly old Riah who cares for her. She calls him her "fairy godmother."

There were no "fairy godmothers" aboard a nineteenth-century British war vessel commanded from afar by the government and administered on shipboard by naval officers who had to carry out government commands whether they liked them or not.

Given the lack, what would happen to a young sailor who willingly obeys shipboard orders, yet is eerily "pure," "innocent," and "incapable of lies"? What if he's totally unaware of what his physical beauty and lack of social understanding might stir up in a homosexually inclined petty officer —even to the point of being blind to possible malice?

This is the setting for Herman Melville's novel *Billy Budd*. Though written at the end of Melville's life, the story is laid in 1797, a time of active war. Once again I turned to *Major Writers of America* for historical interpretation and found this note from Richard Chase, editor of the section on Melville. Chase writes that *Billy Budd* was:

"in part inspired by the 1842 case of the American naval brig Somers...The executive officer who presided over the drumhead Court which meted out the punishment was Guert Gansevoort, a cousin of Melville...and the case seems to have thrown a cloud over Gansevoort for the rest of his life."[5]

Since the case had stirred up controversy over the justice or injustice of the harsh sentence, it's likely that the guilt-haunted Gansevoort talked it over with his cousin Herman Melville, who knew the sea and how men behave at sea.

Melville starts off his tale observing that manhood defines itself by the medical and legal "sciences," a clear indication that empathy in the Victorian era was deemed unmanly. In the story,

5. *Major Writers of America*, Harcourt, Brace & World, Inc., 1962

Captain Vere—fearing for his image of seaworthy manhood—sees empathy as an "upright judge" who allows himself "to be waylaid by some tender kinswoman... seeking to touch him with her tearful plea."

Ditto the ship's doctor: "I doubt its [empathy's] authenticity as a scientific term—begging your pardon again. It is at once imaginative and metaphysical—in short Greek."

Melville likens the sailor boy Billy Budd to Kaspar Hauser, the well known misfit who appeared on the streets of Nuremburg in 1828 and in time was knifed to death. It's evident from available nineteenth-century accounts that Kasper was Asperger. That Melville likens Billy Budd to him suggests that he saw the same social lacks in both boys and was troubled by what happened to them. Melville notes at the start that Billy is no conventional hero, and "that the story in which he is the main figure is no romance."

Billy Budd is an ambiguous tragedy revolving around two unresolved social issues: a beautiful, likeable, oddly immature young sailor who willingly follows the law but cannot grasp the social relevance of what's happening, and a vengeful officer who knows and can manipulate the laws of a war ship but carries the hidden taint of sodomy.

Given Victorian attitudes, it's understandable why Melville may have been reluctant to publish the story. As a man supporting himself as a writer, he had to depend on book sales. His *Moby Dick* was unpopular. Nobody wanted to read such a dark tale, particularly one likening the obsessive drive of big business to Ahab's obsession to kill the whale. Now Melville was writing another tale that might be even more unpopular—one that threw light on two social issues Victorians didn't want to face: the shipping off to sea of boys we would diagnose today as "autistic" and the jailing of men caught soliciting other men. In addition, his story dealt with the tug-of-war between a legally imposed military system and all too human despair.

What we have today is one of the great American classics stitched together from barely legible notes found in Melville's desk after his death in 1891. He had closed his manuscript with the capitalized words END OF BOOK. Did Melville really believe such loaded social issues could be brought to an end?

* * * *

It's 1797. Billy Budd, the incredibly handsome young sailor, is handed over from a home bound boat to the *H.M.S. Intrepid*, a vessel short of crew. He's as good natured as a child—in truth, seems to be yet a child, unfinished as a bud yet to bloom. The old sailor Dansker calls him "Baby Budd." Though Billy can sing, he can't read and write, and under stress, has a severe stutter. He also has, under stress, a speedy and powerful reflex blow when teased with a knife blade.

Still beardless, Billy claims that he was found in a pretty, silk lined basket hanging from a doorknob—a story that implies he was high-born and illegitimate. Or was he told that by those who'd just as soon ship him off to sea? Either way, Melville has written an amazingly apt description of an Asperger teenager, bright in one respect, infantile in another. He notes that:

"to deal in double meanings and insinuations of any sort was quite foreign to [Billy's] nature...he was young, and, despite his all but fully developed frame, in aspect looked even younger than he really was."

Now we come to the character of John Claggart, the master at arms whom Melville describes as "a sort of chief of police charged... with...preserving order on the populous lower gun decks." Gun deck gossip has it that Claggart "volunteered into the king's navy by way of compounding for some mysterious swindle whereof he'd been arraigned at the King's Bench." Though Melville writes elliptically, his words suggest that Claggart's "mysterious swindle" arraignment may well have been sodomy:

"Insolvent debtors of minor grade, together with the promiscuous lame ducks of morality, found in the navy a convenient and secure refuge."

The story of *Billy Budd* has been defined as a classic battle between innocent good and worldly evil: Adam and Satan in Milton's *Paradise Lost*. Perhaps. But between the lines, Melville has also given us a heartbreaking yarn of two social misfits: one a malevolent manipulator and probable homosexual, the other a trusting naïf and probable Asperger. For many nineteenth-century autistics and "sodomites," the only available home was the sea.

There's another detail only hinted at in this story. In times of battle, warships needing more crew took on jailed men. Claggert may have been one of them.

Re-read the exchange between Captain Vere and the ship's doctor over mercy and what constitutes manly behavior. The two of them must have known the charges against Claggert and the temptation that beautiful Billy would stir up in him. When Billy didn't understand what Claggert had in mind, Claggert turned vicious, and Billy struck him a deadly blow. When Billy had first transferred to his ship, Vere was warned that—despite his sweet likeability—Billy could be quick with a powerful blow. And sure enough, it has happened. Given London's warship rules, Vere is stuck with a shipboard hanging and the crew's outrage. The crew knows Billy's a child; they love him as a father loves his son. The captain has his manhood image and British honor to uphold. The crew can't speak up for fear of letting "the cat out of the bag." The cat o' nine tails whip was a British invention used to enforce shipboard discipline; it could inflict appalling agony and lasting scars. Though the "cat" is not mentioned in Melville's story, its threat must have hovered over the crew, silencing them. That leaves Billy trapped: Billy who can't understand what the trial is for, that it will end in his being hanged. Like Arthur in chapter 2, he might know the ceremony of death but not its reality. Melville ends Billy's tale with a ballad lament fashioned, he tells us, by one of the crew. It feels hauntingly right ("Darbies" was slang for manacles).

> *They'll lash me in hammock, drop me deep*
> *Fathoms down, fathoms down, how I'll dream fast asleep*
> *I feel it stealing now. Sentry, are you there?*
> *Just ease the darbies at the wrist, and roll me over fair*
> *I am sleepy, and the oozy weeds about me twist*

The song throbs with the ache of old time blues.

* * * *

Melville's short story, "Bartleby, the Scrivener," also aches; this time not for Bartleby, who seems to be oblivious to what's happening to him, but for his pained and bewildered boss: the old lawyer who tells the tale.

A scrivener is a copyist. In the 1853 days before there were typewriters, a "scrivener" who could hand copy endlessly and precisely any legal or financial document handed him could get steady employment on Wall Street.

English literature professors have interpreted Bartleby's story as Melville's portrayal of his own depression, but all those who call themselves "Aspie" will tell you Bartleby is one of them. Why he resonates so totally with Aspies I'm not sure, only that they're drawn to his politely repeated refusal:

"I would prefer not to."

Though Aspies cannot see that his refusal is life-denying, the old lawyer can:

"What I saw that morning persuaded me that the scrivener was the victim of innate and incurable disorder. I might give alms to his body, but his body did not pain him—it was his soul that suffered, and his soul I could not reach."

Like an autistic child who can only arrange his toys in a meaningless line, Bartleby can only respond by repeating the meaningless phrase "I prefer not to." Words that ultimately bring his life to an end.

But their effect on the old lawyer does not end. Bartleby's "innate and incurable disorder" causes the lawyer unrelieved distress:

"For the first time in my life a feeling of overpowering stinging melancholy seized me."

It's a feeling so overpowering that the old lawyer feels compelled to tell us Bartleby's tale—much as Guert Gansevoort, haunted by his role in the real-life case of the American naval brig *Somers*, must have felt compelled to tell that tale to his cousin Herman Melville.

In two stories, Melville has given us two different characters, each with recognizable traits of autism's social disconnection. Both stories end in a death that the characters appear not to have understood or anticipated. Both stories also involve the bewildered reaction of others.

In Bartleby, the old lawyer tells us:

"My first emotions had been those of pure melancholy and sincerest pity, but just in proportion as the forlornness of Bartleby grew and grew

to my imagination, did that same melancholy merge into fear, that pity turned into repulsion. So true it is, and so terrible too, that up to a certain point the thought or sight of misery enlists our best affections, but, in certain special cases, beyond that point it does not. They err who would assert that invariably this is owing to the inherent selfishness of the human heart. It rather proceeds from a certain hopelessness of remedying excessive and organic ill...

...And I trembled to think that my contact with the scrivener had already and seriously affected me in a mental way. And what further and deeper aberration might it not yet produce?"

The lawyer's distress lingers with us today. Asperger's combination of systemizing skill and social disconnection still makes us anxious. Not as greatly as it did the old lawyer, but running it a close second. Today's society graces autism with the title "special." Though many Aspies have jobs, there are those who hear that word and boast that they are too "special" for daily labor. Social security makes it possible for them to live at home, play video games, compare notes, and share opinions. Though the pattern is less self-destructive than Bartleby's, it is still a form of life refusal.

* * * *

Today's response to autism has progressed beyond the world of Bartleby—sometimes not as much as we could wish, but look at how far we've come. View again the 1565 Breughel picture, painted in a century when burning changelings was taken for granted. Two hundred fifty years later, a biology-trained abbot contacted a Parisian doctor telling him that a runaway boy was not a changeling or idiot but had something wrong with him that deserved medical attention. Another time span and we reach novelist Dickens depicting the cruel "repudiation" of odd children. After him comes Melville, giving us in character detail the bewildered and contradictory feelings that autism can stir up in us, the everyday working folk.

For the most part, acceptance of those less able to deal with life has been due to the poets and novelists who made them human.

* * * *

In the latter half of the nineteenth century, service for the severely autistic was limited to family help and public asylums. Then every so often—quite by chance and to everyone's amazement—individuals would emerge who combined mental limitation with inexplicable genius. Victorian entertainment impresarios were quick to see how they could turn these exceptional beings into theatrical gold. Calling them "idiot savants" (there's that word "idiot" again), they presented them on the concert stage to astound audiences with mathematical and musical tricks.

Such a character was "Blind Tom,"[6] America's first verified account of autism.

Tom was a slave boy from the South, thrown in for free with Col. Bethune's purchase of his mother Charity. He was Charity's fourteenth child, and because he was blind, the slave

6. All of Tom's pictures are from *Learned Pigs and Fireproof Women: Unique Eccentric and Amazing Entertainers*, Ricky Jay, Villard Books, Farrar, Straus and Giroux, 1986

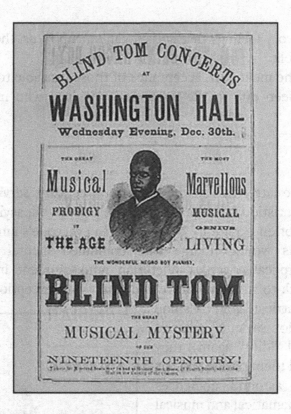

seller considered him worthless. Every day that Charity went to work in the Bethune house, she brought Tom with her. While she labored, he sat in the corner of the parlor listening to Col. Bethune's daughters sing.

It wasn't just that Tom was blind—he wasn't remotely like other children. One story says he spoke in disjointed monosyllables and save for his remarkable musical ability, he was probably an imbecile. Another says he was known for deliberately hurting his playmates, not out of malice but because he liked the sound of their yelps. An old-time publicist writes about his gift of perfect pitch, how by the age of two he could sing the songs the Bethune girls were singing and improvise accompanying harmony. When Col. Bethune purchased a piano, Tom's talent emerged fully, though he was not yet four. Or so they say. Tom's history varies according to who's telling the tale. Bethune, his owner? The local newspaper? Nineteenth-century theatrical impresarios? Early twentieth-century autism authorities?

After rummaging through the internet and a multitude of old paperbacks, I found I liked best Ricky Jay's theatrical account of Tom with all its nineteenth-century concert stage pictures: *Learned Pigs and Fireproof Women: Unique Eccentric and Amazing Entertainers*, Villard Books. Farrar, Straus and Giroux, 1986.

* * * *

Wakened in the middle of the night by the sound of piano music, Col. Bethune, thinking it was one of his daughters, came downstairs. There he saw Tom, age four, sitting at the piano, his feet dangling off the stool, playing his daughters' piano pieces— perfect note for perfect note.

The next day, Bethune called in his musical friends. They played more intricate pieces for Tom, and Tom played them back, perfect note for perfect note. Col. Bethune realized at once that he owned a slave prodigy who could earn him serious money on the concert stage. He hired a piano coach and a theatrical manager, and by the time Tom was ten, Bethune had turned "Blind Tom" into a major attraction on the concert stage circuit. Tom could play any piece he heard; he could stand with his back to the piano and play it, left hand treble, right hand base. Newly constructed railroad lines coupled with local newspaper ads were making traveling acts more profitable than ever. By 1860, Tom was playing for President James Buchanan. Endorsed by Mendelssohn (or so they say), he played the principal capitals of Europe. Bethune was raking it in.

Though Tom's speech continued to be peculiar, he could imitate any sound he heard. Mark Twain writes of sitting across from him in a railway car when:

"...[Tom] began to sway his body violently forward and mimic with his mouth the hiss and clatter of the train, in the most savagely excited way...What a wild state he was in! Clattering, hissing, whistling, blowing off gauge cocks, rings his bell, thundering over bridges... whooping through tunnels, running over cows...He kept his face constantly twisted and distorted out of all shape. When he spoke he talked excitedly to himself, in an idiotic way and incoherently, but never slowed down on his imaginary express train to do it...and then instead of lying down at night to die of exhaustion, [he] was to sit at the grand piano and bewitch a multitude with the pathos, the tenderness, the gaiety, the thunder, the brilliant and varied inspiration of his music!"[7]

In 1908, having been treated well by Col. Bethune, Tom died at the age of fifty-eight. Bethune had made a fortune off him: something in the neighborhood of $750,000, which today would be about $19,000,000. Being blind and autistic, Tom had no social awareness of being black or of his financial worth, slave or free. He adored Bethune who praised him for doing what he wanted. Tom's mother knew that playing piano on the concert circuit was a far better life for her son than picking cotton in the vicious plantation heat. She also knew that he was worth a fortune to Bethune.

Bethune, for his part, knew that a war between the states was about to break out, and if the South lost, the slaves would be freed. Claiming that Tom's success was due to his work promoting him, Bethune extracted a contract from Tom's parents Charity and Domingo that entitled him to the lion's share of Tom's concert profits. In truth, Bethune must have also known that whichever

7. Wikipedia

side won the war, a money contract awarding two ex-slaves would not be honored in a Southern carpet bag court.

Charity, separated from her son for thirty years, was finally allowed to rejoin Tom, primarily to expedite the Bethune family battle over the fortune Tom had made for them. She was given $500 a year plus food and shelter.

* * * *

According to the great Charles Darwin, a "body of well instructed men, who have not to labor for their daily bread" is critical to the development of "high intellectual work" on which "material progress of all kinds mainly depends."[8]

As Darwin's "well-instructed" men discussed material progress, the class on which that progress depended labored on. The doctrine of utility—sprung from the Protestant ethic: "to work is to pray"—continued to command long work hours and minimal wages on both sides of the Atlantic.

8. *The Descent of Man.* 1871

There were no child labor laws. All able-bodied children—
including those with autism—were put to work as soon as they
were big enough to carry a bucket of kitchen slops or scramble
up a chimney. In the cities, that meant sweeping those chimneys,
lugging the coal scuttles, and emptying chamber pots. In the
countryside, it was farm labor. Boys on the autism spectrum
bailed hay and tended the animals. "Naw, he don't talk, he milks

"DISTHRESS !"

the cows." Along with farm work there was heavy railroad labor:
digging and laying tracks— any service where "a strapping young
lad" was needed. Girls, peculiar but diligent, were taught to cook,
bake, churn, sew, embroider—maybe even stitch on the newly
invented sewing machine with its treadle wheel. Overseas sale of
goods depended on shipping, and shipping depended on sailors.
Obsessive Asperger boys could be counted on to "know the ropes."

Then there were the memory-gifted misfits who could recite the Bible, a boon to illiterates. Thus a vast army of anonymous odd ducks was absorbed into the nineteenth-century labor force.

Those incapable of any kind of work or even communication were housed in an asylum, where once in a while an "art savant" would turn up. Since there was little profit in drawings, structures, and carvings, their work was seen only by a handful of visitors— along with an occasional doctor who'd reached the medical nadir of caring for asylum inmates.

Dr. Edward Sequin (an exception?) writes of the work of James Pullen, a talented deaf non verbal housed in an 1885 UK asylum. Pullen's carving skill was exploited by none other than the Prince of Wales who sent him tusks of ivory to carve. (Who profited, I wonder?)

Except for his carvings, Pullen had little to offer. According to Treffert's *Extraordinary People*, Dr. Sequin described him at the age of nineteen as alternately wild and sullen:

"...the pupil who was six months learning the difference between a dog's head and his tail. If spoken to he uttered by no means pleasant sounds, and when corrected he would run away and hide himself if possible."[9]

Dr. Sequin must have wondered how the wild and sullen Pullen could have the visual talent for exquisitely detailed carvings. It was far odder than any fiction a Victorian novelist could dream up.

9. Darold A. Treffert; M.D., *Extraordinary People*, Universe.com Inc., Lincoln Nebraska

7

LATE 19TH CENTURY:
MEDICAL PROGRESS MEETS THE CONCERT STAGE

The reign of Queen Victoria is drawing to a close, the Prince of Wales will soon be crowned King Edward VII, and concert stage audiences have grown weary of savant talent. Savants, they complain, are sulky, imitative, not always attractive in their savant-ness, and invariably male. Novelists, scientists, and entertainment hungry men loosen their collars, light up cigars, and look around for a new brand of enlightened diversion: preferably female.

Enter the charismatic Dr. Jean Martin Charcot at the height of his power at the Salpêtrière Hospital in Paris, presenting in lecture format something more amazing than savants and more alive than painted nudes: sexual ecstasy in the guise of a medical demonstration of a female phenomenon that Charcot calls "hysteria." From his study of the female body, Charcot has learned (he says) that a woman's womb tends to wander about in an unstable state, thereby causing an eruption of precarious emotional instability, hence the term "hysteria," derived from the Greek word for "womb."

Everybody who is anybody crowds into Charcot's Amphitheatre to observe his demonstration. Fly-by-night journalists squeeze in next to published authors. Theatrical stars share seats with demimondaines.

> *"The huge Amphitheatre was filled to the last place with a multico-loured audience drawn from tout Paris."*[1]

In preparation for his medical lectures, Charcot has nosed about the Paris madhouses, taking daguerreotypes of writhing young women in becoming dishabille: hair disheveled, garments sliding loose, their faces recalling the cathedral sculpture of Saint Teresa in a state of religious ecstasy, an angel blessing her.

Next Charcot demonstrates a new version of the old mesmerism, now called hypnotism. He induces a hypnotic state

---

1.   Quote from Munthe, a nineteenth-century Parisian doctor. Source: *The Female Malady*, Elaine Showalter, Penguin Books, 1985.

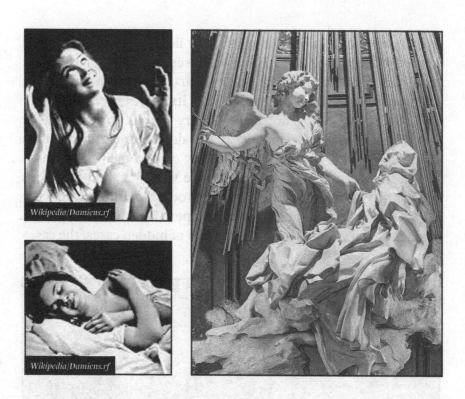

Wikipedia/Damiens.rf

Wikipedia/Damiens.rf

in a "hysterical" woman, sticks pins in her and she doesn't cry, feeds her worms and she tastes pate de foie gras. Then—even more amazing, nay astounding—he induces a hypnotic state in a woman suffering from paralysis of the legs. The woman lets go of her crutches and walks!

The crowd is in ecstasy.

News travels from Paris to Vienna. Though the phenomena of hysteria and hypnotism are not entirely new to him, young Sigmund Freud takes a train to Paris and arrives at the Salpêtrière Hospital to observe Charcot and his hypnotic therapy in action (1885/1886). To his surprise, Freud discovers that Charcot is only interested in exhibiting his female patients and their behavior, not in what they have to say. Freud and his compatriot Josef Breuer have been compiling a record of the rambling stories, dreams, and fantasies patients have told when they lie on Freud's couch and stare at the ceiling (1895). The process seems to awaken thoughts long buried in their dreamy unconscious: erotic nightmares that cultivated Vienna has kept hidden from its well behaved daylight.

The Nightmare, painted by Henry Fuseli in 1787, made Victorian Vienna very anxious. Is the demon squatting on this collapsed woman a male sexual fantasy or a woman's nightmare recollection of rape? What is the horse watching, and why does he look so excited, his nostrils flaring? Today's culture accepts the dark reality of sexual abuse but not upper class Victorian Vienna. Though social workers may have known of hidden cases, the cases would have been denied.

By permitting his female patients to lie on his couch and confide their past to him (permission no other Victorian doctor would have granted a woman) Freud established a process that freed his patients from the shackles of hysterical illness. But the process stirs up a significant social question: Were Freud's patients upper class Viennese of independent means; women who had chosen to come to him and could afford his fee?

Note the clothes on the woman in Fuseli's painting, and the luxurious couch on which she has fainted. Compare that scene to a photograph taken of Dr. Charcot exhibiting a working class "hysteria" patient.

The photo shows Charcot in a top hat and formal suit, grabbing the wrist of a servant class patient in order to display her to his audience. The patient, stripped to a corset and hospital bonnet, turns her face away from him as nineteenth-century servants were trained to do when the master of the house stepped by.

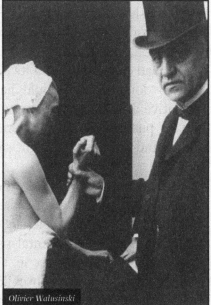
Olivier Walusinski

The Fuseli painting and the Charcot photo show two women who've been invaded, but their stories are quite different. Fuseli's woman is a luxury tale; Charcot's patient is a charity case used in a medical demonstration. If she's been molested, what doctor would bother to listen to her nightmare story?

Freud's upper class patients called Freud's technique "the talking cure" and told the story of their emotional release to friends. Word of mouth sped through fashionable Vienna; and soon men, too, were paying money to lie on Freud's couch and confess to the ceiling. Philosophical and neurological academics gave the process their official blessing—thus giving cultivated Vienna a new way to define identity—one complete with a classic vernacular: Psyche, Narcissus, and Oedipus.

Medical progress had freed itself of the cheap world of concert entertainment. "Psychoanalysis" had been born.

* * * *

Word has it that, at the end of his life, Freud was asked what else he would have liked to have studied. He's reported to have said "I would have liked to have studied neurology." Anti-Semitic Vienna had exiled him from its neurology labs.

No doubt Freud would have been a top neurologist, but a creative and literary bent was also churning in his soul. As he himself put it: "the case histories I write should read like short stories and that, as one might say, they lack the serious stamp of science."

In the eyes of the world, whether science or fiction, Freudian psychoanalysis will become linked to "trauma." "Trauma" implies a psychic wound that *somebody* has caused—and that somebody must be blamed. Judgmental psychiatry will grow to dominate the 20th century autism scene. Until the late 1960s, mothers will be blamed for causing their child's autism. Even then it will take another decade for the cultural lag to catch up.

All this is for later chapters. For now, just follow the process.

* * * *

The patient lies on Freud's couch with only the ceiling as witness, the great doctor sitting out of sight so the patient's thoughts can emerge undistracted by the presence of another human. It's a lonely process akin to a prisoner in solitary confinement tapping on the cell wall in hopes of hearing a signal from another inmate. In this lonely state the patient is to free-associate—one thought tumbling after the other with no apparent relationship. Only the fragmented past as each patient recalls it: the self-pro-

Flickr/roberthuffstutter

tecting lies, the pretense, the small mean cruelties: secrets kept tidily repressed in order to stay alive. It's a process akin to those out of body experiences people describe in near death moments: times when they find they're looking down from the ceiling at themselves lying in bed.

The Gnome. Odilon Redon, 1880

Reality has turned existential and solitary. The patient no longer belongs to a family and community, or the continuities that hold family and community together. Memory is a crumble of momentary details, each solitary moment detached from the other like dots in a painting by Seurat. And startlingly similar to the way those with autism take in reality.

* * * *

News of this new life view will travel from doctor to doctor to become a feature of European mental hospitals; each "alienist" (original term for a psychiatrist) developing his own particular interpretation of the human soul. No two doctors ever quite in accord.

From this body of accumulated thinking, the Swiss psychiatrist Eugene Bleuler will invent the word "schizophrenia": a
portmanteau word composed of the Greek "schizo" (split)—and
"phrene" (mind). It will be a more inclusive and generous spirited
word than the old Latin terms "Dementia Praecox" and "Dementia
Senex": terms declaring unequivocal madness for both young
(Praecox) and old (Senex).

In spite of Bleuler's more kindly word, a welter of opinionated
opinions (depending on who's in power) will continue to swirl
around analysis. Given limited neurological knowledge and the
role of rank, Poe's "fusing power of poetic imagination" is really all
any of them have.

* * * *

Dr. Eugene Bleuler knew his patients as friends, walked
the countryside with them, and was drawn to poetry and literature. When he was still an adolescent, his older sister was
hospitalized for what would be a lifetime of mental illness; and
undoubtedly it determined his professional pursuit. One can't
help but wonder if Bleuler coined the word "schizophrenia" to
protect his sister from the old country belief that "dementia"
was God's punishment. He must have wanted to keep her safe
in a psychoanalytic ward where she'd be sympathetically treated
and studied (as 100 years earlier Itard had studied and cared for
Victor).

In 1908, Bleuler will coin another word, this one from the
Greek word "autos" (self). Since he was known to visit mental
institutions, he must have observed "idiot savants" like James
Pullen; also characters like Melville's Bartleby—patients who were
trapped in lonely self withdrawal. Would his new word describe
them or only those more severely schizophrenic? Would he (or
any doctor then) have known the difference? Bleuler will define

his new "autos" word as *"schizophrenic thinking devoid of logic and reality."*

The word is AUTISM.

The word will lie dormant for thirty years when it will spring to life, subject to a new set of opinions, interpretations, and arguments. In 1924, Leo Kanner, an Austrian psychiatrist, will immigrate to the United States to become director of children's psychiatric services at Johns Hopkins Hospital, Baltimore, Maryland. In 1943,he will publish a medical study of eleven children he's been seeing in his clinic. He will describe how from infancy they have seemed *"cut off from their parents [existing] in their own impenetrable world."* Kanner will be the first American clinician to make the case that their behavior constitutes a unique syndrome that he will call *"Early Infantile Autism."*[2]

But before any of this can happen, there will be two world wars. World War I (the war that was supposed to end all wars) will drain Austria of the "savoir faire" the rich had always traveled "abroad" to acquire; leaving Vienna impoverished, coal a luxury, and Sigmund Freud asking his patients to pay him in potatoes.

In her book *Terrible Honesty*, Ann Douglas writes vividly of Vienna's post WWI destitution and Freud's "impotent rage" as he struggled to deal with cold, hunger, and patients who couldn't pay. According to Douglas it was British associates and patients who kept Freud afloat until—suddenly, amazingly—big money began to roll in. Affluent Americans had caught the psychoanalytic fervor and were flocking to Vienna to be analyzed.

"...writers, editors, poets, artists, playwrights, actors, even cartoonists all fell so hard for analysis that the Village [Greenwich Village] was

2. Richard Pollak, *The Creation of Dr. B*, Simon & Schuster, NYC, 1997, page 250.

soon a hot bed of Freudian explanations for just about everything—and Freud the only authority American writers seem to allude to more frequently than the Bible."[3]

Feeling that his insight into the dark recesses of human nature had been appropriated inappropriately, Freud himself wrote of the insane *"rush of American life with its worship of the almighty dollar, its cheap and manic promises of instant gratification and its prudish middle brow moralizing."*[4]

Despite Freud's dark opinion of America, popularized interpretations of his technique spread rapidly through college towns. Eastern Seaboard intellectuals now attributed all human oddity to an infant trauma—curable by Freudian analysis. In time this would include autism.

Then abruptly Freud was gone. The 1939 news of his death in London created an unexpected gap in the landscape of psychoanalytic opinion.

Mid-Western intellectuals, feeling they had lost out on the immediate Freudian experience, began to hanker for their own guru: a learned intellectual whose psychoanalytic know-how would top that of New York. Their hankering would create the perfect setup for Bruno Bettelheim—due to arrive in Chicago in the middle of WWII. Chicago will acclaim him as Freud's true heir, the brilliant new authority on that most difficult and rapidly emerging human oddity: autism.

Bettelheim's interpretation of autism will spring from Leo Kanner's interpretation. Though Bettelheim will contribute little new insight, he will profit from writing pop psychology books and magazine articles on autism. Even more telling, he will understand the value of appearing on that blazing new post WWII personality

3. and 4. Ann Douglas, *Terrible Honesty*, Farrar, Straus and Giroux, NY, 1995, p 121.

driven product: TELEVISION. His televised interpretation of autism will sweep the country—putting into active play Freud's disgruntled opinion of America.

But before any of that can happen, there will be World War II.

8

WORLD WAR II

Our country entered WWII on December 7, 1941; and in response to the instant surge of American patriotism Hollywood's shoot of the film *Casablanca* was sped up. With the exception of Humphrey Bogart, Dooley Wilson, and a few bit parts, the film cast was European; many of whom had barely escaped the Nazis. According to Wikipedia: in the scene in Rick's café where the French drown out the Germans by singing the Marseillaise (one of the all-time great movie scenes), the cast wept for real. They had found their way to freedom, and the U.S. had joined the fight. It wasn't just a movie scene: it was the turning point of their lives, and of Europe's future.

The 1940s was also my turning point; a decade so deeply tied to my growth as an individual and the mother of an autistic child that I am including it in the following chapters—for here my history with my daughter Temple merges with the history of autism.

****

In September 1941—WWII still hovering uneasily on the American horizon—I, age fifteen, am stowed in a girls' boarding school nestled safely in the Massachusetts Berkshires. We're late blooming lilies coming into bud in a sheltered garden where no weedy passions would be allowed to take root. Gone from the school encyclopedias are the pages on human reproduction. Even the porter's "drink and lechery" speech in Shakespeare's *Macbeth* is mysteriously missing.

But there's no way to expurgate what is happening politically. Radio and Miss Lyons' Current Events class tell us the truth straight out: Germany has taken over Czechoslovakia, Hitler is broadcasting his next invasion intention, and American radio comics are imitating his demanding shriek: "I want peace, I want peace, I want a piece of Rumania!!" Miss Lyons assigns us the newspaper editorials. Even when we're too lazy to read them, there's no escaping the point of the newspaper cartoons mocking Britain's Prime Minister Neville Chamberlain who's waving his umbrella and calling out: "Peace in our time." Then in rapid succession, Chamberlain—the symbol of appeasement—is voted out, Britain elects Winston Churchill, and President Roosevelt prepares the United States to join Churchill in the battle against Hitler.

But that doesn't mean that everyone in our country is for Roosevelt and his "Lend Lease." Each schoolgirl falls in line with the political beliefs of her family and hometown: the east coast girls are for Roosevelt; the midwest girls are isolationists. Heated arguments break out in Miss Lyons' Current Events class until she insists that we behave civilly to one another and allow both sides their right to speak.

Then suddenly there's December 7, 1941, and Pearl Harbor. East-West arguments vanish. Like it or not, we're a country at war. Miss Margaret, our headmistress, ushers the entire school into the main living room to hear Roosevelt declare December 7th "a date which will live in infamy." The next day, we gather again in the living room to hear Churchill's action-rousing words: "we shall fight in the fields and in the streets, we shall never surrender."

Everyday life changes abruptly, even school life. From that day on, the trains taking us home for vacation run late, packed with U.S. soldiers in transport to Europe. No seats are available. We ride home sitting on our suitcases and flirting with the soldiers. One of them flirts back—then suddenly in a last minute need to reach out to a girl before being flung into battle, he says "If I write you, will you write back?"

"Of course." At that, he hums the pop song "Paper Doll."

"You'll be my paper doll?"

"Yes."

His name is Mitchell Ramonas, and he writes me letters from Europe. Then the letters stop, and I get a letter from his mother. He's been taken prisoner, she writes, and is in a German army camp. Please, will I keep writing to him, they say the letters go through. I never learn if my letters go through; I never hear from him again.

Despite the intrusion of war, our boarding school goes on exchanging dances with Deerfield Academy, a nearby boys' school (the teachers frantically signaling us to keep a distance from our dancing partner, fearful lest our cheeks seek out the pimply jaw of a Deerfield boy). There's one senior: a strapping 6-foot-3, whom the boys call "Tiny." The next year, a top form boy asks me if I remember him.

"Yes, of course."

"Tiny's dead."

There it is. War so immediate it's hard to digest: that the boy I'm dancing with be might be the next, that he's thinking the same and wants me to know it. The top form Deerfield boys all have draft cards in their pockets. Boarding school is no longer a sheltered garden.

Due to the war my family moves to Cambridge, Massachusetts, where my father works for the Boston branch of the War

Production Board. Though I'm still in boarding school, during the summer break I talk my way into a Harvard Summer School art course taking place in Harvard's Fogg Art Museum. I treasure my daily walks across the Yard, haunt the Fogg's galleries, and secretly love the Pre-Raphaelite paintings the museum docents consider too second rate for public display. They've hung them out of sight on the student staircase leading to the studio where we copy old drawings.

But the painting that leaves me stunned is Picasso's *Guernica*. It hangs alone in the Fogg's vast echoing stone hall. New York's MOMA must have shipped it to the Fogg for duration safekeeping. Each morning I go into the hall and stare at it, transported by its war horror: mythic, political, and screamingly human.

Alamy

One morning in that summer of 1942, a rumor spreads through Cambridge that Prime Minister Winston Churchill is here on a secret visit to give the States the fervor to fight side by side with the Brits. Though the visit is classified hush-hush, gossip whispers everywhere that he will speak in the Harvard Yard. Harvard is an official wartime Naval Training Post.

On the rumored day the Harvard Yard gates clang shut, guards standing at attention. No one is allowed in without a pass. Somehow—I don't remember how—my sister and I wangle passes. Once through the gates, we find the Yard already packed with Navy men wearing white officer dress uniforms and lined up in rows, their stiff, white officer hats like so many peppermints. There's also a milling crowd in a roped off section. We're not the only ones who have wangled passes. We push our way through the crowd, squeeze up the jammed steps of Weidner Library, and shove ourselves into a niche next a stone pillar. From our hard won perch we can see across the Yard to Memorial Chapel, built to honor the men killed in WWI. Suddenly a spotlight stronger than the sun lights up the steps of the chapel, and there stands Winston Churchill— his bald head shining in the spot, his words from the old litany rolling out to us from the speakers attached to the trees:

"Till we have beat down Satan under our feet…"

He finishes to a roar of applause; the Navy band strikes up "God Save the King." (England had a king in WWII). Next comes the "Star Spangled Banner." Side by side with England we sing both anthems and weep.

There are war facts yet to learn, hidden facts. No thrilling figure in a spotlight, no celebratory band, no newspaper editorial to let us in on the significance of Freud's 1938 departure for London, arranged by his daughter Anna. No radio broadcast to tell us that his four sisters are in a concentration camp, due to be exterminated. We don't even know what a concentration camp is.

* * * *

In 1944, I graduate from boarding school and enter what is still Radcliffe. There I discover I'm well prepared academically, about fifteen years old emotionally, and in competition with English Lit. majors so adult, so bright, so articulate, I can't figure out if we've read the same assigned story. Then on April 12, 1945, sobbing girls gather in knots to share the news that Roosevelt is dead. Grief makes us equals.

* * * *

1945: That summer Lt. Richard Grandin came home to Boston on military leave after fighting in France in the Battle of the Bulge. VE day had declared the end of the European war, but the Allies still had Japan yet to conquer. In August President Truman ordered the bombing of Hiroshima, next Nagasaki, and on September 2, 1945, World War II was over.

We saw the atomic bomb as a miracle. None of us saw it as sin.

* * * *

In the break between VE day and VJ day, Lt. Richard Grandin and I—caught in the triumphant mood of a war drawing to its close—sprang unprepared into each other's arms.

In that charged-up moment, I had no way to understand the inference of what Dick told me that first night home on leave: how his battle with anxiety—and the fury it could stir up in him—must have played into his report on the colonel—and how in time I, too, would come under the lash of that ferocious anxiety.

The Battle of the Bulge was one of the worst in WWII. The cause for war had become irrelevant; both sides were fighting to stay alive. According to Dick's lieutenant report to the higher-ups, the American colonel was sending men into unnecessary danger causing 50% battle casualties. The higher-ups agreed to relocate the colonel to a less crucial war zone, but Dick didn't see it as sufficient. He wanted the colonel (a West Point man) officially dismissed; his military career dishonored. When Dick wouldn't let up, the commanding officers said they would transfer the colonel as agreed—but they would also transfer Dick to a less crucial unit. When Dick told me all this, I thought his denunciation of the colonel was brave.

After we were married, I realized it was a repeating pattern brought on by acute anxiety: a pattern I would come to know by heart. I think Dick found ambiguity in any form terrifying, and autism is always ambiguous. His solution for our daughter Temple was to declare her sub-human and demand she be put into an institution. When I'd try to explain—slowly, carefully, step by step—how to manage the current problem with Temple, he would shout me down: "Just say it in words of one syllable!"

I never could. Each problem—as with all autism and war problems—was too complicated, too ambiguous to be solved by shouting. Now further enraged, Dick would ram home his opinion of me in a tirade fit to cow the bravest soul. And I wasn't brave. Unlike the commanding U.S. army officers, I had no army procedure to fall back on.

I imagine Dick thought— if he could think at all in a state of high agitation —that shouting would return him to the moment he'd been in before the ambiguous "something" happened. But the "something" *had* happened, and like it or not we'd have to deal with it; generally with some sort of compromise. And that led back to ambiguity. So my solution was to accomplish the compromise in secret. Not a good solution, but in the years we were together, it was the only one I could ever think of.

****

In the middle of WWII, penicillin came into medical use. That meant more wounded G.I.s could survive the battlefield. But in order for them to survive, doctors had to focus on the battle-damaged amputation, ignoring the unconscious soldier whose leg they were sawing off. It was hard boiled, that compartmentalized thinking, but as we've all learned from viewing *M*A*S*H*, it was the only way the doctors could keep themselves intact emotionally. Let penicillin and nurses do the work of healing the amputated leg.

When WWII was over and doctors returned to civilian practice, the old war habit of separating thinking from feeling was so entrenched that they continued to see their job in terms of isolated body parts—heart, liver, kidney—forgetting the human who housed them. And seventy years later we, their patients, would still accept the pattern, visiting one "specialist" for one body part, another for another. Each of our visits would then be reported to what we would term an "internist": a catch-all title for the doctor we once called "our family physician."

Somehow the medical world will have convinced us that we deserve no better and we, in turn, won't know how to achieve better. Doctors, hand in glove with drug companies will have programmed us into accepting "specialized" medicine. And "specialists," while listening to our tale of woe, will keep their multitask eye on the computer, the great "virtual" specialist.

Compartmentalizing would also permeate autism. Our "special" child, as we would call them, will be handed about from pediatrician to bio-neurologist, speech pathologist, Special Education teacher, Autism Behavior Analysis expert, and so on. For the endless array of specialists, parents will mortgage their homes.

* * * *

After witnessing the death of thousands of G.I.s, General Eisenhower, newly elected USA president, put through the G.I. Bill of Rights: a post-war bill that would entitle those who'd survived the war to have the best education the country could offer. James

Conant, then president of Harvard, was against the bill, convinced that a bunch of loud mouthed G.I.s would change the character of Harvard.

And they did.

They also changed me. I recall a 1947 class on International Relations. It was the year the professors said, "Harvard is in no way co-educational except in fact," and I was pregnant with Temple. The class was full of Veterans, not college kids but men in their late twenties and early thirties, men who'd left a leg behind on an international battlefront, men who'd faced the worst, were afraid of nothing and weren't about to swallow Harvard whole. At this particular lecture one Vet got to his feet, stopped the professor in mid talk, and yelled out his challenge: what did the professor actually know about the international scene, where was he getting his information? Other Vets joined him. I stared at these men—their crutches, their empty sleeves and trouser legs (Charles Bolte). One man had an eye patch (Cord Meyer). I didn't know it yet, but those Vets were the first glimpse of the "beat" generation: the under-ripple of challenge that would culminate in the 60s anti-Vietnam rebellion. I watched, I listened, unaware that I was absorbing their fervor. If they could challenge established authority, so could I.

* * * *

Today I wonder if Dick could have understood that having an autistic child was a challenge, not a dishonor. There were moments when he almost understood, weeks at a stretch when he saw Temple as a little girl he was fond of—a child he yearned to be a good father to, and get it right. Then there'd be other times when he'd revert to repeating almost mantra-like, "If someone will just tell me what to do, I'll do it." I was never sure who that "someone" was, but whenever I didn't measure up, he had a second mantra, one he'd deliver in a commanding yell, "That's not the way it's supposed to be."

Could I have been wise enough, brave enough to wait out that second mantra and say again what I felt we ought to do for Temple? Could I have understood that hiding information was not a solution, but a postponement? I didn't. I couldn't. He didn't, he couldn't.

It was 1949. Standing in the way were the words exchanged with the Viennese doctor to whom Temple had been assigned.

"It is autism," the doctor said in a sibilant accent that sounded like a war movie Nazi villain ,"Infant schizophrenia."

In a flash Dick picked up the words. In a flash the doctor turned on him:

"No, no, no, I did not say that. I said that she manifested autistic symptoms."

What did it matter? "Symptoms" sounded ambiguous, and Dick wasn't going to allow ambiguity to trip him up as it had in the Battle of the Bulge. Eugene Bleuler's "schizophrenic thinking devoid of logic and reality" was solid ammunition.

* * * *

What none of us knew yet was that the Beats wouldn't be the only post war change. In New York City, ex G.I.s, equally brave, equally ready to challenge the establishment but with a different mindset, were cooking up a scheme for promoting business. Something they would call "Madison Avenue." Flavored with G.I. slang, "Madison Avenue" would reshape post-war books and magazines; and set the stage for television. Television would introduce us to Dr. Bruno Bettelheim. And Bettelheim, in a guttural Viennese accent oozing *Freudian know-how*, would deliver his verdict on autism:

"Infantile autism is the most severe, ahhh, psychotic distur-
bance of childhood, ahhh known to man ... everybody wants him to
be dead as the Nazis indeed wanted all the Jews to be dead."

9

AUTISM AND THE MINEFIELD OF BLAME
1940s–1950s

As noted before, 1943 was the year that Viennese psychiatrist Leo Kanner described in a medical paper eleven children he'd been seeing in his Johns Hopkins Baltimore clinic. From infancy, he wrote, these children appear to exist in their own impenetrable world, cut off from their parents. Kanner was the first clinician in the U.S.A. to make the case that the behavior of these children constituted a unique syndrome that he entitled "early infantile autism." In addition—and more significant—Kanner declared that autism was a schizophrenic disorder caused by an infant trauma that could only be understood and resolved through Freudian psychoanalysis. At the same time—and curiously at odds with this declaration— Kanner was also considering the possibility that autism was neurological. That he chose to pronounce it psychological rather than physiological may have been due to the 1940s infatuation with "Freudian explanations for just about everything." In the 1940s and 50s, American magazines, plays, and movies were all featuring hero psychiatrists who could straighten out any life problem a writer could dream up. Except, of course, the problem of autism.

We parents accepted the notion that autism was a social disorder, or—as the media put it to us—a "psychosocial" disorder; but we had no idea what "psychosocial " meant or even what "infant trauma" meant. And we sure didn't see ourselves lying on a doctor's couch and telling our dreams to the ceiling. Never mind. This is how you knock out autism and we better pay attention.

In the accepted Freudian mode Dr. Kanner told us that environment had caused an infant trauma, and environment was the home. Parents of autistic children, he declared, were "highly intelligent, self-absorbed, preoccupied with their careers and emotionally cold, keeping their autistic children neatly in a refrigerator that did not defrost."

Us? How? Didn't Dr. Kanner know that only college degree parents understood psychoanalysis and only rich professionals like the professors at his own Johns Hopkins could afford his fee? As for refrigerator chill: when a judgmental "headshrinker" (we knew that term) tells you to your face that you're emotionally cold, even a fellow professor might turn icy.

Fathers were let off the hook. Mothers were to blame.

A decade and a half later Kanner would regret his interpretation, and publicly absolve mothers at the first national autism meeting in 1969; but it would be too late. Blame had been let loose, swept into high profile with an assist from author Phillip Wylie. In his popular book *Generation of Vipers* (1942, republished in 1955): Wylie created the term "momism." Though today it's hard to read him with a straight face, from 1942 through the 50s, Wylie's words carried a vicious punch:

"Mom is an American creation...a middle-aged puffin with an eye like a hawk that has just seen a rabbit twitch far below. She is about twenty-five pounds over-weight, with no sprint, but sharp heels and a hard backhand which she does not regard as a foul but a womanly

defense...She smokes thirty cigarettes a day, chews gum, and consumes tons of bonbons and petits fours. The voracity of a hammerhead shark, which cannot see what it is trying to gobble but never stops snapping its jaws..."[1]

Wow! How could any mother, aunt, or girl swallow such guff? 1942 was wartime. There were no bonbons. Sugar and butter were rationed. Women worked in factories. (Remember Rosie the Riveter?) We teenagers were assigned hospital jobs as soon as we got out of high school. Nevertheless, though we were proud of our jobs, as soon as WWII was over, we handed them back to the men, hurried home to don aprons and acquiesce. Even then, in spite of our girlish attempts to win male approval, psychologist Erik Erikson, (who coined the word *identity*) agreed with Wylie. In his *Childhood and Society*, published in 1950, Erikson told us that Mom assumes authority on the mores and morals of her home, her community:

"yet she permits herself to remain...vain in her appearance, egotistical in her demands, and infantile in her emotions."[2]

Wylie and Erikson were imprinted on us. When I became a first time mother, I dreaded the thought that I might turn into Wylie's "Mom" and impose my unwanted self on my child. Still a child myself, I didn't understand that my newborn infant needed my total embrace. Instead, out of a vague yearning to be a "good" mother and avoid "momism," I interpreted my baby's lack of response as a sign that she found my embrace "intrusive" and wanted me to leave her alone.

So I did.

1. Farrar & Rinehart, New York, 1942
2. Erik H. Erikson, *Childhood and Society*, W.W. Norton & Co. 1950

In those early post war years, did any of us young mothers know what our babies wanted? Few babies were born in WWII; the men were off fighting. I'd never even held a baby, let alone thought about raising one.

We were all of us in the same boat. The difference was: my child had autism. She couldn't respond.

While other mothers played peek-a-boo with their baby, my baby didn't even grab for my beads and stuff them in her mouth. While other babies cooed and babbled and their mothers babbled back, my baby was non verbal. Whatever it is that makes mothers and babies respond to each other, it wasn't in my baby.

Was she trapped in her "own impenetrable world?"

Though autism was still relatively infrequent, there were other mothers with children who lived in the same strange world that my child lived in—children who were much more difficult than mine. Yet in an odd fashion, all of them fitted the syndrome Leo Kanner had described. Did other mothers think that their babies were snubbing them? Had they, too, tried hard not to fall into the pit of Wylie's "momism"? Had our nonintrusive behavior made our children worse? Did it account for Kanner's opinion that we'd kept them "neatly in a refrigerator that did not defrost"? Unsure of our maternal role, and fearful for our children, we were ready to believe any opinion handed to us. The stage was set, the timing was perfect.

Enter Dr. Bruno Bettelheim, the ultimate psychiatrist, with his black rimmed spectacles and heavy guttural rumble, with his brave life experiences facing the Nazis in Dachau and Buchenwald, with his *Freudian expertise* straight from Vienna. We adjusted the rabbit ears on our new TV sets and viewed him, trembling.

"*It is a psychosis*," he tells us, the TV studio lights glinting off those scary spectacles, "*caused by the children's frigid and unloving mothers...*"

"Oh no! Not us again!"

"Ah—you ask."

"Yes, you" chimes in the entire medical profession. Already in accord with Kanner and his Freudian "psychosocial" talk, doctors everywhere were quick to champion Bettelheim and blame mothers.

Wait a minute! Hold it! There must be an authority with a good word for us. It would take a decade for that authority to speak up: one Bernard Rimland, a PhD in psychology and father of an autistic boy.

Rimland's challenge would ride on the old division between those who study *how* something works vs. those who study *why* it happens. Bettelheim and the Freudians were all so sure that autism was the result of an infant trauma that none of them had stopped to wonder *why* the exact same behavior pattern was turning up in a variety of children who had each (according to the Freudians) suffered a different psychosocial trauma.

Rimland would look for the *why*; and in time will prove to the Freudians that autism is not the result of a wounded psyche but of a faulty physiological wiring. He will discard the term *psychosocial* and give us instead *bio-neurological* (a term we still use today). Until that time, Bettelheim and the Freudians would continue to rule, but not as totally as they felt they deserved.

Among those already questioning them were the stoic New England Puritans.

"We don't lie down on couches and tell people our troubles. We stand up and face them."

New England believes that education is the key to understanding—even understanding a condition as baffling as autism. I look back on those years, and gratitude for my New England upbringing sweeps over me. So much so that now seems like the right time to detail Temple's early life—the years when we both learned and progressed.

* * * *

Early on I realized that hope—real hope—is a bet. You check out the odds and place your bet. Though I had yet to find reliable odds, I'd heard Temple humming the Bach melody I was playing on the piano: a little two part invention. Even though she was ignoring me, even though she stared past me with her strange eyed stare, even though she sat with her head drooping—playing with torn newspapers instead of toys—she'd heard the melody and was giving voice to it. Was it echolalia or communication? Since the word echolalia hadn't been invented, I bet on communication.

It took a second incident to back up the bet. I'd brought Temple to Dr. Bronson Caruthers, director of the Judge Baker Guidance Clinic, at Children's Hospital Boston, for help. After the first appointment, Dr. Caruthers asked me if the hospital clinic could keep Temple in the research ward for a week of observation. Not really knowing why—it was 1949 and Temple was only two—I said yes. Even though I was scared—even though the hospital staff could barely manage to get Temple through the electro-encephalogram (EEG). Even though they had to fasten my child down with some kind of baby restraint to still her thrashing, medicate her to turn her sobs into drugged sleep and me hovering over her, singing, soothing, trying to act the mother role in a wrenching scenario. Even in in spite of all this, I trusted Dr. Caruthers. Not just because of his expertise, but because of him. Where does trust come from? How do humans make the trust connection?

Wait. There's more to the story.

Though Dr. Caruthers said I could visit Temple every day of her weeklong visit in the research ward, I would only be allowed to observe her through the one-way window in the playroom door. That night was the night of the big weep: such hard sobs I thought I'd strangle on my own tears. The next morning I woke up exhausted, unable to think. Then in an odd flash I saw how tears could stop thought. If I was going to hang onto my hope bet,

I'd have to forego tears and think. That flash has stayed with me, sending and resending me on missions to understand—not just how to help my child but how the phenomenon of autism and its relationship to us actually works.

The first report on Temple's hospital visit came from the nurses caring for the children in the research ward. They said she seemed to be happy but was aloof; more beguiled by the red crib she slept in than by the other children.

Next I went to the ward playroom with Dr. Caruthers; and together we watched Temple through the one-way-window door. I saw how she ignored the other children; sat apart from them, playing by herself in the same old style I knew so well. This time she was playing with scraps of note paper; and one of the scraps slid under the door. Dr. Caruthers pushed it back with his foot. Temple saw it come under the door and returned it. Dr. Caruthers pushed it back again, and again Temple returned it. She didn't keep the paper to play with, she engaged in the exchange. "She connecting" Dr. Caruthers said. *As she had connected with the Bach*, I thought. Connecting would be key.

After the week was up, after the EEG proved there was no retardation (the term then used), no brain damage, and no epilepsy, Dr. Caruthers diagnosed Temple: "She has autism." I sat there wordless; my dream that hope was a bet didn't fit anymore. The poet John Dryden began to sing in my head, his rhymed couplet taunting me with its translation of Ovid:

> *"Work without hope draws nectar in a sieve*
> *And hope without an object cannot live"*

Not until 1965 would I—or anyone—find that much needed object.

* * * *

In 1965, EEG testing would reveal a bio-neurological link between epilepsy and autism: part of the indisputable proof that autism was not psychosocial as Kanner had diagnosed in 1943 and Bettelheim was still endorsing, but bio-neurological. Had Dr. Caruthers already sensed this back in 1949? When he told me that Temple's strange stare might be small epileptic seizures, did he also have a hunch that autism and epilepsy were connected? Is this how the neurological dots coalesce into hope's needed object?

Whatever Caruthers thought, we were both relieved that Temple had no "retardation," no brain damage and no epilepsy.

"I think she's going to talk" Caruthers said, "but let's speed up the process. Mrs. Reynolds teaches children who have trouble learning to speak."

There it was again: Education, that old New England standby.

Relief swept over me. I could breathe, I could think. He gave me her address; I got out my notebook.

Mrs. Reynolds had a small, home grown nursery school where she taught speech and group behavior to young children who couldn't manage either. Temple went to Mrs. Reynolds for three years, three times a week, three hours each time. Right from the start, she wanted to talk, but it took her till she was nearly five before she could master it. Mrs. Reynolds also taught Temple the basics of nursery school: how to sit in her chair and wait her turn. It was Temple's introduction to awareness of others, their needs, their struggles: an awareness all children have to learn.

That June, as she approached five years old, Temple finally mastered speech. Mrs. Reynolds felt that she could now go to a little summer camp for special children run by Mrs. Huckle. Mrs. Huckle was British and indomitable; she'd been director of a school on the French Riviera for the sons of Maharajahs and could improvise on any social challenge that came her way (which may have included her own wartime escape from Vichy France). I loved her imagination, her verve, her courage. She looked Temple in the eye and said:

"Temple, you may come to my camp, but at the end of the summer you must have learned two things. You must learn to recite the Lord's Prayer (no easy task for a little girl who'd just learned to talk) and you must learn always to do your veddy, veddy best."

The Lord's Prayer has two valuable life rules. First: ask only for today's bread: "Give us *this* day our daily bread." Don't worry about tomorrow, just today. Next: when you ask to be forgiven for a wrong you did, first forgive the person you think has wronged you.

In response to Mrs. Huckle's second instruction: Temple has always done her "veddy, veddy best."

* * * *

At the end of the summer, Mrs. Huckle felt that Temple was ready to join a regular kindergarten if the local day school knew her history. I talked to Everett Ladd, the principle of Dedham Country Day School and to Mrs. Dietsch, the head of kindergarten through third grade. The two of them agreed to accept Temple provided we all worked together as a team. (Where there's autism, teamwork between family and school is essential.) Temple entered kindergarten in 1952 and soon learned that class routines were consistent, and she would be expected to follow them. Because of my daily exchanges with Mrs. Dietsch, whatever didn't go well at school, I knew it. And whatever didn't go well at home, Mrs. Dietsch knew it. That's how Temple learned consistency and expectation.

Mrs. Dietsch also taught the other children how to help Temple—and except for occasions of fatigue and noise, Temple flowed along with them—slowly becoming aware of *their* needs, *their* struggles, *their* games. "If I don't play the games by their rules, they won't let me play with them," she said. Since she wanted to play with them, she was happy to learn the established rules of dodgeball and hide-and-seek.

From 1950 to 1965 Temple and I were both counselled by a Freudian trained Austrian doctor who—like Kanner and Bettelheim—had also emigrated from Vienna but had chosen to live in Puritan Boston and intern at Children's Hospital. In those fifteen years Temple, the doctor and I changed: each of us taking responsibility for what life was handing us. The story of our time together involves the nature of character. Though much of it is neural, some of it is familial and cultural, and some rides on what happens daily. Genes determine our physical look, body type, and neurological tendencies. That much we're stuck with. But we also have gene promoters that respond to what's called "external experience," and "external experience" is what the day offers us. How we respond to the day depends on how—and what—we have responded to before. Character is cumulative. As Abraham Lincoln put it "After forty, a man is responsible for his own face."

****

The Austrian doctor and I meet in 1950. He tells me that Temple has been psychotic, "but now she's beginning to pull out of it and become neurotic." "Oh," I flip. "Like the rest of us?" He's not amused. In his high, sharp Austrian accent he explains that the difficulty I have with Temple's father is because we're two different psychological types. He refers to me as a hysteric. I look the term in my Freud book and learn that it means I'm a woman who wants a penis. Oh Lord! Is that really what he thinks? I've wanted a lot of things in life, but not that! The doctor says when Temple reaches sixteen, she will have to undergo psycho-analysis "to find out what ze trauma was." I look up "trauma."

Uh oh. Sounds like something I've caused. Is that what he and Temple talk about? All Temple tells me is that she sits in the chair opposite his desk, eats M&M's, and goes to the bathroom. The doctor says the bathroom is a sign of anxiety. I know that much already. Anxiety has also taken root in me.

Years slip by. Temple says, "I never tell the doctor anything important." He's not after her childhood secrets; he's watching the changes in her behavior—puzzling over them—sorting them out. "I do not understand why she got ill," he remarks abruptly. "And I do not understand why she is getting well?" Is he talking to me or himself? Has he stepped away from his role as psychiatrist and connected as a friend? Two friends looking for ways to understand what's happening? He quotes a phrase of a fellow psychiatrist, a phrase he particularly likes. "She calls it 'ze will to thrive.'" He thinks that's what's connecting Temple to the world.

Yes, Temple wants to thrive. *Don't we all*, I think? *Thrive and come to terms with what life throws at us.*

Does the doctor know about Bettelheim? He must. Why has he never mentioned him, never asked if I've read his articles or seen him on television? Perhaps the doctor feels—since Temple's progress is positive—what is to be gained by discussing him.

Or perhaps—and here's the real question: is the doctor, himself, struggling with a gnawing suspicion that "Freudian explanations for just about everything" may not be the explanation for autism? Is he searching through Freud's publications for evidence that Freud worked with traumatized children (or any children)? Since there's no such record, where did Kanner get his notion that "early infantile autism" was trauma caused, treatable only by Freudian psychoanalysis?

When Kanner first embarked on his career in Vienna, the psychoanalytic culture there was controversial and competitive. Opinions and theories were filched from earlier doctors without giving credit, or even seeking proof. Had this approach rubbed off on Kanner? Did he dream up his "trauma" diagnosis on his own or was it already circulating? Either way, why would blaming parents for causing an infant trauma help an autistic child to connect?

Temple's doctor has interned under Bronson Caruthers, the doctor with the New England character and belief in the value of education. If Caruthers has left his mark on me (and he has), he most likely has left one on his young Austrian intern. When he ordered the EEG tests for Temple, did he share with his intern his hunch that autism was neurological not psychological?

I see the scene playing out like the Truffaut movie scene between old Dr. Pinel and young Dr. Itard. It's 140 years later; the scene is now between an old Puritan doctor and a young Austrian doctor. Each doctor, independent of the other, has concluded that autism is not caused by a trauma. Old Dr. Caruthers has backed up his hunch via an electronic system. The young Austrian doctor has gained his through a growing empathy for Temple. Two ways to explore the nature of autism. Both valid, both concluding that autism is not caused by a trauma. If that's so, where does it put Kanner and Bettelheim and the much promoted Freudian psycho-social kingdom?

Perhaps Temple's doctor has good reason not to talk about Bettelheim.

* * * *

Bruno Bettelheim's story also begins in Vienna.[3]

In the lull before WWII, Bruno has set his star on becoming a Freudian analyst. But as Fate would have it: just as his first year at

---

3. The following account is based on *The Creation of Dr. B*, author Richard Pollak, publisher Simon & Schuster NYC, 1997.

the University of Vienna is concluding, a family death forces him to forgo getting a degree and run the Bettelheim lumber business instead. For this Bruno will never forgive Fate, nor will he forgive her for his bad eyes and ugly face.

In spite of this blow to his Freudian hopes, running the family lumber business turns out to be short lived. In rapid sequence glass shatters, the Nazis take over, and Bruno finds himself interned in a concentration camp. There his bad eyes work to his advantage (along with a little bribery). Too blind for hard labor, he wins indoor work mending socks. Ten months later, through moneyed pull, he sails directly for New York in 1939 before WWII is fully underway. Here Fate takes another up-turn and drops him into a Chicago University enclave where awe of Freud reigns in equal proportion with envy of eastern seaboard intellectuals. With his heavy Viennese accent and Freudian lingo, Bruno rapidly attracts Chicago attention. So, figuring the Nazis have destroyed all record of Jewish intellectuals, he gives himself a refreshed vita of psychoanalytic degrees. Four years later, when Leo Kanner introduces autism to Chicago, Bruno announces that he is an expert in this field. Awed and delighted, the University of Chicago appoints him head of its Orthogenic School, the institution where Chicago parks its difficult young. Money pours in and before you can believe it, Chicago ceases to tip its hat to the highbrow east. It now has its own living embodiment of Vienna and Freud.

Just one nagging problem: Bruno's command of Freud is limited to 101 Psych at the University of Vienna and a single year of analysis. Needing instruction in both Freud and autism, Bruno hires Emmy Sylvester, a Viennese he's met in Chicago. Sylvester is an M.D. from the University of Vienna and a certified American psychiatrist. Warm and stylish, Chicago sees her as the "diva" of psychoanalysis. She joins the Orthogenic School, teaches Bruno the psychoanalytic view of autism, and co-writes with him the pop magazine articles that guarantee him national media endorsement.

Alamy

It's the 1950s. Parents of autistic children now read every word Bruno publishes. He's their hero. But again there is a nagging problem: he yearns to be their *only* hero. A quick clash of wills with Sylvester; she's forced to depart, and voila! Bruno with his Viennese accent and scary black spectacles is free to interpret autism all by himself.

Meanwhile, back at in the dormitories of the Orthogenic School, life is far from happy. Eric Schopler—who has come from Vienna to Chicago for the sole purpose of studying autism therapy under Bettelheim—says he's seen more than he wants to see of Bruno's cruelty to children and therapists. Most of all, his cruelty to young, frightened mothers.

As soon as he can claim his doctorate, Eric Schopler leaves Chicago for the University of North Carolina. In 1972 he will start his own school there and teach parents how to be co-therapists for their children. Called TEACCH, an acronym that stands for "Treatment and Education of Autistic and Communication related Handicapped Children," Schopler's school will, in time, lead the way in autism therapy.

Eric Schopler is not the only one to disapprove of Bruno Bettelheim. Though it's still only the 1950s, the social climate of the entire country has begun to shift. Mothers are less sure they deserve to be demonized, and fathers agree. 1956 is the year that Bernard and Gloria Rimland's son is born with autism. Rimland, a Ph.D. in psychology, has been trained to believe that psychosocial forces are the principal cause of mental illness. But he and Gloria— along with their family doctor—are convinced that Mark's rages and dislike of being touched don't fit any known pattern of mental illness. Remembering something they both learned in Psych I,

Bernard and Gloria burrow among the old textbooks stored in their garage, open them up, and flip through their tattered pages. Yessir! Here it is! "Early Infantile Autism." The text offers enough clues to spur Rimland and his cohort Benson Ginsberg to undertake the neurological research that will lead in time to Rimland's book *Infantile Autism: The Syndrome and Its Implications for a Neural Theory of Behavior.*

Though the book won't be published until 1964, a media fight with Bettelheim begins when Rimland states publicly that autism is an organic disorder and should be treated like diabetes or cretinism.

The following dialogue between Bettelheim and Rimland is on record:[4]

Bruno: If autism is neurological, how come my Orthogenic School achieves an 85% reversal of the disorder?

Bernie: Where's your evidence for reversal?

Bruno: I have an 85% cure rate!

Bernie: Let's see your record. You have no hard evidence? Yet you're not ashamed to shame parents. Shame them so severely that we [he and Benson Ginsberg] can't get a straight story out of them. Give me what you've got. And I don't want to read any cute vignettes.

Bruno: The literature needs revision.

Bernie: I hear the Ford Foundation wants statistics. You took their money. What are you going to tell them?

Bruno: Until the literature on autism is revised, I give out only behaviors.

Bruno finally allows that autism might have a neurological source, but its neurology would be compatible with his psychogenic

4. Richard Pollack, *The Creation of Dr. B*, Simon & Schuster, NYC, 1997.

hypothesis. He's not alone in his view. Erik Erikson notes that even if autism should turn out to be "constitutional," it might still require psycho-therapy.[5]

OK, says the general public (meaning us moms), but how do you define (or practice) psychotherapy? Is it lying on a couch and telling your story to a psychiatrist who is seated where you can't see him, or is it sitting up and talking to him face-to-face? Temple and I have gained from the face-to-face guidance of Temple's doctor, who's a licensed psychiatrist and who has probably undergone the couch variety of psychoanalysis himself. Does that make his counseling "psychotherapy"? If so, how do you grade the counseling of Temple's teachers who are trained educators but have no formal psychoanalytic training? Is one "therapy" more authentic than the other? Or is one individual better than another at figuring out how to make life work for a child on the autism spectrum?

In 1964, Bernie's book will finally be published and parents will be grateful. Nevertheless, Freudian practitioners and the publication industry (ever ready to guard their cultural turf) will brush his book aside and go on accusing mothers. Some mothers will never recover.

Where did it go —-the old medical rule: "First do no harm"?

5. Erik Erikson, *Childhood and Society*, Norton 1950.

10

HONOR AND SHAME IN THE 60s

In the 1960s, our country was trapped in a savage and pointless war with Vietnam that had begun in 1955 and wasn't to end until 1975. Outraged young men burned draft cards and civic blame turned murderous. In November 1963, President John F. Kennedy was assassinated. In April 1968—three years after his Selma March —Martin Luther King, Jr. was assassinated. Two months later, it was Robert Kennedy.

For me, the 1960s and the Vietnam War are linked forever to the gunshot death of my sister's oldest boy, Peter, a seventeen year old with traces of autism. He's in my thoughts so often that I must include his story.

Too young to have a draft card, Peter joined the Marines dreaming that the Vietnam war would grant him a passport to heroic manhood. He was critically wounded fighting in the jungles of Vietnam where he and a Vietnamese boy shot each other: the accepted ritual to the manhood they each longed for. My sister and her husband flew to the army hospital in Vietnam where Peter, still alive, had been brought by helicopter. They managed to fly him home and to a U.S. hospital where for months he battled to stay alive with no working body parts left inside him. Only gut determination hauling him upward to the light, and a feral urge to prove himself a hero.

Peter got his hero wish. He was buried in his marine dress uniform. A full Marine Honor Guard of boys his own age blew taps as they lowered his coffin into its grave and handed my sister the now folded American flag that had covered it. The sun was unbearably bright; an icy wind whipped us.

The burial over, we gathered at my sister's house in that strange boozy mélange of wake and celebration. The next day with one of my daughters, our arms wound round each other, we took our exhausted, grief sodden selves home by train.

Today my son's closest friend is Vietnamese. Each of them has three sons; the six boys have grown to manhood together and to this day are still close friends. When they were little, I remember them frolicking in a swimming pool. Playing war.

There's little use looking for reason in human behavior—let alone the behavior of those with autism. We honor civilization with the same fierce spirit that we smash it up. Emotion rules, intelligence justifies—and we seem to be unable to come to terms with the two.

As for honor, it would be years before I could accept the role it played in the fraught politics of the 60s. How it would continue to play out, even in the sport little boys invent: games where honor is for heroes, shame belongs to the coward.

Looking back at WWII, I rethink how Temple's father fought in a tank in the infamous Battle of the Bulge. How he undertook reconnaissance—searching out the enemy, protecting the safety of his men, acquitting himself with courage and holding fast to his sense of honor. When WWII finally ended, all he wanted was to come home and live a peaceful life. It never crossed his mind that he could father a child he would see as less than perfect, nor had he envisioned how her behavior would overwhelm him with shame—as if his little girl's autism were something he could fix, as once he'd secured the safety of his men. Autism cannot be fixed in the way that men like to fix things; it can only be lived with. And no man gives another man a medal for that.

* * * *

In the first decade of the twenty-first century, a popular magazine will publish an article about Arthur Miller and his unacknowledged son Daniel, born with Down syndrome in the 1960s. The article will take Miller to task for institutionalizing his son and withholding the information from the public. When I read the article, I had the uneasy feeling that the author had enjoyed shaming Miller; and I wondered if she'd ever experienced an imperfect child. More important: was she old enough to have lived through the 1960s and its conflicted social code?

About five years before Daniel Miller was born, (Temple would have been thirteen) I began research for a TV documentary on what was still called "retardation." To start me off, a pediatrician took me to a top medical school class. One hour's instruction: that was all a 1960s medical student got on developmental impairment. "Because," the pediatrician said bitterly, "no medical student wants to specialize in 'retardation'; there's no money in it." As a result, few 60s doctors knew the difference between developmental impairment and autism. Both conditions were a blank; both pointed to an institution.

Given those terms—and no doubt at the urging of doctors— what choice did Miller and his wife have but to put "Danny" into the Southbury Training School, a private institution about fifteen minutes from where they lived—near enough so they could visit him weekly? Southbury had been founded in the 1930s. At that time it was a top state-of-the-arts facility with 125 buildings on 1,600 acres, housing woodshops and greenhouses. Its purpose then (and today) was to integrate into the surrounding Connecticut community those children who could be integrated, and for those who couldn't, there would be a warm, protected, self-contained community appropriate to their life ability.

Now in his 50s, "Danny" has long since left Southbury to live on his own; and the article will admit he has a meaningful life. So, was it fair to take righteous pokes at Miller like a gull pecking at a live crab that's trying to scuttle free—only Miller is no longer alive and can't scuttle free? What does a millennial writer know of the 1960s stigma against those we then called "Mongoloid"?

Though the Southbury School would have its good years and bad years, in the 1960s, it was far and away the best setup for the socially imperfect. In that decade, most of the mentally impaired—along with the autistic, the brain damaged, and the malformed—were herded into nineteenth-century public buildings, their facades looking vaguely academic (white pillars and brick) inside a catch-all for Mother Nature at her most careless. Institution staff worked as best they could, often teaching the less impaired how to care for the more impaired.

In the light of today's invasive social media, I reread the article, and it dawned on me that what really put the journalist on her high horse wasn't Miller's decision to house Danny in the Southbury School, but his decision to conceal his Down syndrome son from journalists like her. Miller had come so far as a dramatist; it had earned him millions, but it had its price. How could he introduce his "innocent" son ("innocent" is an old-fashioned term for mental limitation) to a clever Madison Avenue marketer whom he himself had finally managed to deal with? His experience would have warned him exactly how the media with their ever-hungry photographers and journalists would hover over Danny, quiz the neighbors, the institution staff, take pictures, and carry off hunks of his family privacy. Would envy and spite take a chomp? OK for him, he could survive it, but what about Danny? Who would be positive? Who would be negative? Who would glorify Danny in order to take Miller down a peg? Did Miller envision Danny's confused delight over public attention, all the while not understanding how and why he's been turned into a public object to be bought and sold in a market where everything has a price? Wasn't a quiet, anonymous life in Connecticut a better choice?

Today celebrity parents with autistic young have to cope with much the same invasive publicity. And with today's social media, it's probably harder. Yet solutions for autism and the mentally limited have often moved ahead because of publicity. Assisted living arrangements have proliferated; special education has become more available. Though far from perfect, families are no longer trapped in the social and medical confusions of the conflicted 60s.

* * * *

To clarify for myself and get a firmer grip on the 1960s confusion between autism and mental limitation, I reread and relived my research notes on visits to state institutions housing those called "retarded."

My notes describe a throng of children raking leaves in the grassy quadrangle of a nineteenth-century building. Some of them are Down syndrome, some are microcephalic. They cluster around me, happy to have the tedium relieved by a visitor from the outside world.

I climb the institution steps, pull open the heavy door, and make my way to a central room. There, I'm greeted by a guide who calls out. "Hey folks, we got a visitor." The crowd calls out in return: "Hey nursie" (every female stranger is "nursie"). "Take my picture." "Come see me." "What's your name?" They sit in bunches, wander the room, sprawl on the floor: a mix of oddity and every day. Over and over, one style or another, they hand me their loneliness: "Nobody comes to visit me." "Nobody sends me candy." Their loneliness troubles the staff: the empty farewells, the families who wave goodbye and never return, never even bother to explain. Do they think because their unwanted ones are intellectually impaired that they don't understand emotional abandonment? As if their feeling selves were as limited as their intelligence?

Actually, how limited was their intelligence—in those years when we didn't know the difference between mental impairment and autism?

I recall a lantern-jawed doctor who was the medical director of one of the institutions. After he guided me through a ward of the seriously malformed (nature can make appalling mistakes), he led me to an alcove and introduced me to his son. The boy, about ten, was sitting at a drawing board, an attendant beside him. He looked up but didn't speak, nor did he appear to recognize his father. Yet his face and demeanor carried no look of intellectual impairment. Today I wonder: was the doctor's boy actually autistic? If so, what 60s medical authority in a remote New England town would have recognized it? For that matter, did the doctor himself know? Or had he simply accepted the diagnosis of mental impairment, along with the advice to institutionalize his son? Then applied to the institution for the position of Medical Director so he could stay close to his boy, make sure someone set him up with a drawing board, so he'd have some kind of stimulus that would help him grow? At least the Southbury Training School had greenhouses and woodshops. Here in this state institution there was next to nothing; a well-meant nothing, but still nothing. Had the doctor himself bought the drawing board for his son? I never saw another one in the institution.

The doctor wasn't the only parent struggling to get services for an offspring diagnosed as retarded. I recall a father who wanted his teenage daughter included in high school classes:

"Just let her be with her own age and learn what she can." Then I recall a mother whose teenage son *had* been included. "But no one bothered to teach him," she said. "They just let him sit there and promoted him through high school. Now he wants to pump gas, but he doesn't know how to read and write, so he can't make out a receipt."

I'm no expert, but I knew even then that these young people were autistic. I also knew—had the cards fallen differently—Temple might have been in the same bind. Or perhaps, with a little better diagnosis, she might have been included in an early work-in-progress autism ward. The next year, when I was undertaking research for a documentary on autism, I saw such a ward.

The room was filled with autistic children between the ages of three and eight, each sitting alone, silent (I've never forgotten the silence of that room), and "stimming," i.e., meaningless repetitive action like rocking and head-banging. I turned to the psychiatrist in charge. "Why aren't these children in school?" I asked. The psychiatrist saw my shocked face. "Please don't write about autism," she begged. "We don't know what it is, we don't know what to do about it. You will only hold out hope and there is none."

That's where autism was in 1962.

Even today I struggle with the thought of what might have happened to Temple if she hadn't come under the care of Dr. Caruthers and his Austrian intern. Over and over I imagine how she could have ended up playing with scraps of paper in a work-in-progress autism ward, non verbal among other non verbals.

Thank God it didn't happen. Not only because of Dr. Caruthers, but also because of Mrs. Reynolds, Mrs. Huckle, Dedham Country School and the Viennese doctor—all of them kindhearted, forwardlooking professionals. Due to the good fortune of their help, Temple's childhood has been fulfilled.

But there's adolescence yet to come, and Dedham Country Day School only goes through the sixth grade. That means Temple will have to leave her familiar world and go to a teenage school. Adolescence is difficult for all children. Everyone gets a new body, new clothes, new friends, and strange new sensations. The changes are worse for an adolescent with autism.

In a misguided attempt to play her old childish pranks in a new school, Temple locks a girl in the broom closet. During gym she mixes up everyone's clothes in their lockers. She thinks it's funny; the girls don't. They treasure their new clothes and now they can't find them. One of the girls passing Temple in the corridor hisses "Re-tard," and Temple strikes her with a book. Yes, her antics have been outlandish. Yes, she's been difficult in the extreme—but did she deserve what she got?

That evening the family phone rings and like all 60s teenagers, Temple rushes to answer it. It's the school headmaster:

"YOU," he yells at her, "are a menace to society! Don't come back after Christmas vacation!" And he slams down the phone. How do I know that's what happened? Temple gasps it out in mortified tears.

"He didn't even ask for my side of the story. He just hung up."

It seems the girl Temple had struck with a book went home and told her mother. Her mother called the headmaster, and the headmaster took his wrath out on Temple. No, it wasn't the school for Temple, but a headmaster who deliberately humiliates an autistic student because she's caused a schoolgirl spat is the real menace to society. To attack *any* adolescent's fragile hold on selfworth is monstrous.

What mattered now was to help Temple to a quick recovery. Besides, I had no way to retaliate. When I voiced outrage to the neighbors, they told me how wonderful the headmaster was—how kind he'd been to allow Temple to attend his school "seeing as how she's autistic." The way they said it signaled their intention. Though they'd included Temple when she was a child, now that she was an expelled adolescent, they would shun her.

I knew I'd have to get Temple out of the community before that could happen—and by a lucky coincidence I'd just completed a year's research for a WGBH TV documentary on autism—in particular on residential high schools for autistic teenagers. During the year I'd learned that there were a number of such schools from Maine down through Rhode Island; and most of them were top notch. There it was again: New England's belief in education.

"Never mind," I said to Temple. "We'll visit three schools I think are great, and you can pick out the one you'd like to go to." After what had happened, I wanted her to have a hand in choosing her own destiny.

She chose Hampshire Country School with its farm, its horses, and cows, and it turned out to be exactly right. Temple herself has written about it. She and I both benefitted from the wisdom of Henry Patey, a wise headmaster skilled in understanding autism. Much of his wisdom I try to pass on today to other mothers—in particular, a piece of advice that applies to all adolescents: how to keep a balance between unconditional love and unconditional acceptance.

As soon as Temple entered Hampshire School, she stopped studying. She loved the school and said so; loved the horses, loved riding them and caring for them; but refused to study. "Why?" I asked Mr. Patey. "She's always been a good student." After what had happened, I needed to know where and how to draw the line.

"Don't worry," Henry Patey said. "Let it go. It doesn't matter if she loses a few years. When she gets through adolescence, she'll come back to studying." But he didn't let her off the hook. In return for excusing her from studies, he held her to expected tasks: she was to feed and groom the horses, clean their stalls, and put down fresh hay. Whether she studied or not, she was to attend all her classes, come to all school meals, school assemblies and group entertainment. His point: unconditional love is not unconditional acceptance. Unconditional acceptance can veer into indulgence. Though I agreed with him in theory, it was hard in reality. When was it her autism that couldn't carry out a request? When was it a teenager hiding behind the excuse of autism?

Today I know there's no precise answer; there are only choices. But choices can be changed, rules readjusted, and exceptions figured out. The trick is to create a new setup with a consistency and expectation that an autistic teenager can manage. Then add in an enticing challenge. Often autistic teenagers can do more than they think they can.

It would take Temple six years to complete four years of high school; she graduated from Hampshire Country School just as the 60s were winding to a close. As I sat at her graduation ceremony, watched her step up proudly and receive a diploma she'd earned by studying hard and honorably, I thought of my final meeting at Children Hospital seven years earlier—right after Temple had been expelled. At the time, I'd wanted Dr. Caruthers to know what the headmaster of that high school had said to her; and I wanted it on record that Temple would be attending Hampshire Country School. Not until I arrived at that 1962 meeting did I learn that Dr. Caruthers had retired and a new staff was in charge; all of them Bettelheim-indoctrinated.

The staff sat themselves at a long table, their notebooks poised, their pencils sharpened; and indicated that I was to sit in the chair facing them (Like a prisoner applying for parole?) The verdict didn't take them long: I was incompetent; Temple should attend their clinic-based school where (as they put it) "We can monitor her."

"Monitor" is not a kind word. At Southbury, Danny Miller was cherished. And the medical director at the institution where his autistic son was diagnosed as developmentally impaired clearly loved his son and had given him his best.

You think I don't love Temple? I brooded angrily as I faced this eerie "superior" team? *Not one of you has given thought to Temple's happiness—nor indicated any concern that she might be scared of your "monitoring" and homesick for her happy childhood. Worse yet: might fear you're punishing her for whatever it was she did that made her a "menace to society!"*

Fortified with what I felt deeply—what I, too, had worked hard to learn, I rose to my feet, told the Bettelheim experts that Temple was going to Hampshire Country School, picked up my coat, and left. To this day I don't know what they wrote on the hospital record—save that I was an unsuitable mother and the Judge Baker Guidance Clinic was no longer responsible for Temple.

Did Temple's Viennese doctor know about this meeting? Probably not; he'd long since finished his internship and developed his own practice. I only know that I couldn't have raised Temple without his counseling and friendship. Though I understood the autocracy lurking in the Bettelheim point of view, it hadn't occurred to me that I might need the doctor's protection from it. Not until an odd incident brought the need home to me.

I spotted him—looking small and anxious—standing in a line-up for a popular movie. He was in the act of beckoning to an even smaller old lady, (a mother? an aunt?) drawing her close to him in the jostling line, so he didn't see me. Nor would he have wanted to; sharp winds were whipping his hair and dignity. *That's how he must have looked*, I thought, *fighting to hang on to his family and his entitled spot in the line of those escaping Nazi Vienna.*

Up till then, I hadn't thought of him as an Austrian Jew forced to flee for his life. My mind's eye had seen him as a psychiatrist officiating at his desk or perhaps a skier—lithe and blond—slaloming down the experts' trail. How did he escape, I wondered—Switzerland maybe? From Switzerland to where? From that 'where' to here? Or was there another country before he and his family could reach Boston, learn a new culture, and build a new life? Temple and I have travelled only the easy road of privilege. Could we survive what the doctor has survived? Stripped of rank and dignity, standing in an escape line with nothing to hang on to but hope and luck? And still have "ze will to thrive"?

* * * *

It's January 1962. Out of the blue I get a call from the doctor asking me to come to his office. He stands to greet me, his head slightly tilted, his odd quirky smile not there.

"Mrs. Grandin, are you aware that Mr. Grandin has been keeping a notebook on you for the past three years? That he is planning to take you to court as a mentally unstable mother, gain custody of your four children, and put Temple in an institution?"

I sit, shocked.

"I do not like to testify in court. But I have done it before and I will do it for you." He asks me if he may talk to the family counselor Dick and I have both been seeing.

"Of course."

Later I learned the two doctors had met privately and agreed that—given Bettelheim's medical authority in 1962—Temple's father might well win legal custody of all four of my children and institutionalize Temple. To block any such action, they'd summoned Dick for a joint session. There, they told him that if he undertook a court case against me, both doctors would testify against him. Faced with their double psychiatric clout, Dick did not dare take action.

But it was a close call—even for the doctors.

* * * *

Cultural change is finally in the air. Though Rimland's book *Infantile Autism: The Syndrome and Its Implications for a Neural*

Theory of Behavior doesn't attract the media attention as do Bettelheim's publications, it soon becomes the leading guidance manual for parents with autistic children.

In 1965, Rimland, at parents' urging, forms the AUTISM SOCIETY OF AMERICA, soon shortened into the acronym ASA. Together with Benson Ginsberg and Eric Schopler, the three men plan the first ASA meeting and invite Kanner to come as an honored guest.

The meeting takes place in 1969 at the Sheraton Park Hotel in Washington D.C. 400 ASA supporters gather together to endorse and register autism as a known bio-neurological disorder. Leo Kanner, visibly old and fragile, formally exonerates mothers, declaring that as early as 1940 he had suspected there might be an organic basis for autism. Bruno Bettelheim does not attend.

It all happens on the day that the astronauts land on the moon.

A few weeks later, Eric Schopler presents a formal paper to the American Psychological Association symposium in Washington. Because there is no clear understanding of autism, Schopler writes, therapists—eager to maintain their psychoanalytic authority—have found it easier to assume the popular view and blame parents. Bettelheim's technique, he opines, is essentially a form of scapegoating parents.

* * * *

In 1990, Bruno Bettelheim will down a handful of sleeping pills with a glass of whiskey, pull a plastic bag over his head, and end it all—finally beyond the reach of further opinion. Today his stained story and our country's faith in it read like a misguided sidebar in the social history of medical practice.

It was no sidebar in the 1960s. Despite established bio-neurological proof, "Freudian expertise" (Bettelheim wasn't the only one practicing it) would continue to insist that autism was a trauma caused by cold mothering.

But was it actually Freud's expertise? I searched the internet and could find no evidence. Instead I found Freud's wonderfully oblique observation about Bleuler's different psychological terms. (The early doctors all knew each other.) Freud said Bleuler had created a cluster of terms: *schizophrenia, schizoid, autism, depth psychotic.* He called the cluster Bleuler's "happily chosen term ambivalence" (Wikipedia). Freud's teasing remark implied a shared reluctance among the early doctors to define over precisely the disturbances they were studying—or what had caused them.

Not so in the 1960s, and even not always in the 1970s. Bettelheim was gone, but "cause" and its partner "blame" were with us still. The zeitgeist was not yet ready to concede that there might not be a precise answer to autism. Or even an explanation.

11

ANXIETY AND CHANGE

How do you explain the color red to a man who's colorblind? He doesn't know what you see, and you don't know what he sees.

"It's not so much that I'm colorblind," the man said. "It's that I'm color confused. If you show me a box of crayons, I can see the red and blue ones. It's the in between colors. The other day I thought I bought a light blue backpack, but it turned out to be lavender. The same goes for blinking traffic lights. Are they red or yellow? Do I come to a full stop or slow down and proceed with caution?"

That's about how the 1970s saw autism. Though Rimland and the A.S.A. had left their mark, Bettelheim-style judgment was still lurking in the zeitgeist. Though we mothers knew that autistic meltdowns weren't personal, what we couldn't manage—even when we explained autism to the community—was why public meltdowns still upset the public, and the public continued to blame us. Madison Avenue had declared the 70s a decade of social challenge for women. Now the question was: what kind of women were we supposed to be? What kind of mothers? What kind of example? And for whom?

The 70s was a decade of options—all slightly askew. The only way to recount those years is with stories. So here they are. Make of them what you will.

Josh's Story

Both joy and anxiety were roiling around in Josh. He was twelve, had autism, and lived in Dodge City, Kansas. Before we met, I knew Dodge City only from the movies. When I found myself actually there and looking out my hotel window, I understood why Westerners get homesick when they visit the tight landscape of New England. A Dodge City man admitted to me (a little shame-faced) that New England with its prim houses perched on narrow roads choked with second growth trees, made him long for the open sweep of the prairie "where you can stand on a matchbox and see tomorrow."

Josh and I met at a dinner for families with autistic young. After dessert he sprang up from his chair, pulled on a wig, and treated us all to a karaoke show—spinning as he sang, first on his feet and then on his back. Blond and in ecstasy.

"I like rhythm," he announced when he finally sat down, snapping his fingers from the recollected joy. "It's like alcohol. Once you do it, you can't stop it." *Alcohol? Where did a twelve-year-old pick up that one? Had he had experience with alcohol or was it just his sing-song way of describing a momentary high?* Aloud I agree with him and tell him of my own nights of band singing. Driving home after late night gigs hollering songs at the top of my lungs, the music ringing in my head. I tell him he reminds me of Carly Simons' song "Music Is a Natural High."

"Yes, alcohol, that's addictive, but it's good for you. You do it, you just can't stop it." *Is he talking about his own joy or something he's witnessed?* He sighs happily; then after a moment says, "Music makes me lose control. I hear a really good song, I just dance,

dance, dance. But still, it kind of makes me feel out of control."
He squirms in his chair, ecstasy churning indigestibly with the way
he thinks I might think he ought to behave. Though intelligent
and articulate—at ease with a word like "addictive"— achieving a
balance between exuberance and decorum keeps him in a constant
state of jitters. Not just at a dinner of families where decorum
doesn't matter, but at school where it matters a lot.

Weighing heavily on Josh (as I was to learn) was his latest
mismatch with a new schoolteacher and his permission to call his
mother when he has an anxiety overload. The permission stated
that whenever he had a new teacher, he was to bring a written
note from his mother explaining his need to phone home. Well,
sure enough, it wasn't long before he found himself in a state of
jitters—and here's where the two stories of what happened don't
match.

According to Josh, he informed his new teacher that he had
to call his mother. According to the new teacher, she held out her
hand for the permission note which Josh had forgotten or lost or
crumpled into a ball during his anxiety attack. In the interests of
an orderly classroom, she said, "Sit down." But as soon as Josh
sat, anxiety snarled at him like a junkyard dog. He leapt up and
told the teacher he absolutely HAD to call his mother. The teacher,
fearing for her new won authority, commanded SIT DOWN!
That's when—according to Josh—anxiety opened its jaws and
sprang for his throat. He HAD TO ACT. So he took off his baseball
cap, wrote on the visor "Josh has permission to call his mother,"
signed his mother's name, put on his cap, went back up to the
teacher, leaned over her desk so she could see the words, and said
"Read the hat."

The story made the rounds of the faculty who were used to
Josh and laughed.

Not so the new teacher; she actually thought Josh's mother
had written the permission, felt tricked, and let it be known to the

faculty in a burst of justifying (which entertained the faculty even more). The episode goes to show how fast decorum in any form can fall apart, particularly if the protagonist is an inventive autistic fighting anxiety.

TEMPLE'S HIGH SCHOOL STORY

All through the 1960s, Hampshire Country School—nestled among the New England hills—had sheltered Temple from any major challenge. Her high school years there had also included summer breaks at the remote Brecheen ranch in Arizona. Anne Brecheen, the sister of my second husband, was a wise teacher/librarian who sensed intuitively how to counsel Temple through her struggles with social know-how. Where Hampshire School had introduced her to farm life, Anne introduced her to ranch life. And Temple has worn ranch wear ever since.

Nevertheless, as the 60s morphed into the 70s, Temple found herself in the grip of anxiety. She was a senior at Hampshire School; she'd buckled down to studying and had achieved good grades. Now she wanted to go to college; but when she thought about taking a college entrance exam, Josh's junkyard dog bared his teeth. And for good reason. Her father told her he'd written to Henry Patey (the Hampshire School headmaster) stating that her high school diploma was meaningless; that as soon as she graduated, he intended to place her in an accredited institution for the intellectually impaired.

What Temple didn't yet know was that Henry Patey— with her father's letter in hand—had climbed into the school truck and driven a half hour to his long-time friend Frank DiPietro, president of Franklin Pierce College. Frank DiPietro was a small, scholarly man who'd devoted a lifetime to academics. Henry Patey was a large man, respectful of academics but harboring an old farmer habit of gambling on when to take the seedlings out of their sun-warmed cold frame and plant them in the chilly New Hampshire soil. According to my *informed imagination* (a phase filched from John La Carre) their meeting looks to have gone something like this:

DiPietro: (reading the letter from Temple's father) This "accredited institution" is an up-scale home for the retarded!

Patey: Recommended to Temple's father by the mother of an intellectually impaired boy. The mother had German measles when she was pregnant with him. Her son couldn't talk, so she sent him to Temple's speech teacher.

DiPietro: That's proof that Temple's retarded?!

Patey: Doesn't quite hold water. Even—thank God—for her father. All Temple's years with us at Hampshire School he's sent her the *Wall Street Journal*.

DiPietro: Does she read it?

Patey: Loves it, quotes it. Quotes it accurately.

DiPietro: (letter) So how did he come up with this?

Patey: Intellectually Temple is capable of college. Socially she sees herself as much younger than she actually is. Acts younger. Her father mistakes that for intellectual impairment. He's also picking up on her latest fear. The thought of college—and what will be demanded of her—has forced her to realize that the comfortable, comforting Eden she's living in is temporary. The real world is fast approaching, a world where people—even when they're kind and polite—require you to do the work they've assigned you and expect you to carry it out or face the consequences. In this case, the work is a college entrance exam. Frank, she can't do it—not yet. She's immature socially. You're asking a nervous eight-year-old to get out in the middle of a highway and flag down a cop.

DiPietro: Don't think I could do that at any age! (pause) What makes you think her father will pay for college?

Patey: He will when your Dean of Admissions writes a formal letter to him announcing her acceptance into Franklin Pierce. He's a proud man. I know him. Intellectual impairment is apt to be familial...And that doesn't throw a good light on the Grandin heritage. College has a better ring to it.

DiPietro: Can she keep up academically?

Patey: Top drawer. And we won't mention waiving the exam?

DiPietro: What about anxiety?

Patey: Your acceptance will go a long way to curing it... Nothing succeeds like success...Frank, I've gambled on kids whom other schools have thrown out—and they've developed into fine young men.

DiPietro: That's the farmer in you, Henry. Always gambling on the crops...(letter) How will I explain this to my dean?

Patey: We'll fill him in. I told Temple if she makes it into Franklin Pierce, she's to come back to us once week for social and emotional guidance.

DiPietro: You'll keep in touch?

Patey: Of course.

DiPietro: Now the only obstacle is my board of admissions.

Patey: Tell 'em the truth. Tell 'em every young autistic needs a champion: someone who'll go to bat for 'em. Right now Temple needs two champions—or...(indicates letter)

DiPietro: No no—not that. Never that...OK, we'll waive the exams.

Patey: Thanks, Frank. (They shake hands.) We'll give it the old college try.

Between them they did. And it worked!

TEMPLE'S M.S. STORY

All through her college years, Temple studied hard, returned once a week to Hampshire Country School for guidance, and graduated from Franklin Pierce with top honors. Now she wanted to go to Arizona State University for her master's but couldn't do the required math. Once again she needed champions, and this time her champions turned out to be the Franklin Pierce dean and the Arizona State University Board. Between them they arranged for Temple to take a substitute course.

Autism needs champions, but champions need to understand what the role may entail. Henry Patey and Frank DiPietro were knowledgeable friends. DiPietro respected Patey's assessment of Temple's capability. Arizona State University (ASU) and the Franklin Pierce dean had no such connection. The ASU Board, like others before them, wanted to champion autism but had no idea what they were committing themselves to. Temple finally achieved her M.S., but at an emotional cost.

The first cost was social: When she joined the students sunbathing around the swimming pool, they either ignored her or picked up their towels and left. Never before had she been openly snubbed and it hurt. She called home. I suggested a shrink, she said, "No—you're a better shrink than they are. Besides, they all talk." She knew she was being gossiped about and it made the hurt worse. All she had to left hang on to was pride in her academic work.

But who at ASU was checking on her academic work?

When the faculty finally discovered that for a year and a half Temple had been writing a thesis on cattle behavior in feed lots and different types of cattle chutes, they told her the topic didn't fit their academic requirements. It was a subject for an agricultural university.

Right there lay the crux of the problem. Apparently, no authority had checked on Temple's topic. If they had, they would have seen that her work was valid and would have helped her transfer to an agricultural college where she'd get full credit, and no time lost. Now it was too late. Temple had accomplished the major body of her thesis and wanted ASU to quit stalling and credit it. ASU, fearful of how they'd look in the eyes of other academics, held back. Finally, grudgingly, the Board decided they'd *have* to give her credit. They knew she was autistic when they'd accepted her; and that made them beholden to Section 504 of the Rehabilitation Act passed in 1973: the first piece of civil rights legislation to specifically address the rights of people with disabilities.

Did the students know what was going on? Probably. Gossip travels fast in an academic town, often hurtful. Did Temple understand the legal bind the faculty was in? I doubt it—and here's why:

Like Josh in Kansas struggling with the invisible idea of social suitability, Temple in Arizona was struggling with the invisible idea of academic suitability. Worse yet, academic suitability was riding on an equally invisible *academic principle*. The purpose of the academic principle was to uphold the agreed-upon *academic rules* (also invisible). And the academic rules were up against an invisible law: Section 504 of the Rehabilitation Act.

To Temple none of this was "real." Her work with cows was real—as anyone with eyes could see. Can invisible rules look at you with reproachful eyes? Show you a wounded hoof?

Though she may not have grasped why she was academically and socially out of favor, the pain of the double rejection was as real as a cow's wounded hoof.

THE WOMEN'S LIB STORY

In spite of growing neurological knowledge and the dazzle of emerging electronics, most of the 1970s culture was still trapped in old social barriers. Autism was still a trauma-caused disorder, curable only by analysis; and women were less intelligent than men.

Though Arizona State University had granted Temple her M.S., and Temple was making a name for herself designing cattle equipment, she still had to battle the professional scene on her own. Despite the women's rights movement and Betty Freidan's book *The Feminine Mystique*, the 1970s prejudice against professional women was very real. Slaughterhouse workers did their damnedest to destroy equipment Temple had designed and installed. Not because it was faulty, but because she was a woman.

In the 70s, all women were trapped.

For me the trap happened over a credit card. Women could use credit cards only through established male credit. Proof of this barrier came about when I and one of my other daughters took a plane to visit a university she was applying to. I had reserved a rental car at the local airport.

When we went to pick up the car, the rental service said they wouldn't release it unless I gave them a credit card number. I said I didn't have a credit card; I would prepay with a check which they could verify through my bank. They said no. If I smashed up the car, a credit card would be the only way they could recover full car value.

"Why didn't you tell me this when I reserved the car?"

"We assumed you'd bring your husband's credit card."

The university undergraduate interview had been on the calendar for months; my daughter and I had come a long way. Snow was starting, and gusts of it were slamming against the oil smeared windows of the rental office. We needed to get to a warm motel room (also reserved). So I did what all 70s women had to do.

At top vocal pitch I announced the name of a university professor and my personal connection to him.

"Give me your phone (no cell phones in the 70s), I will call him, and you will rent me the car."

That did it. They knew they'd accepted the car reservation without stipulating a credit card. Since their business depended on the university, they didn't want a top professor pointing out their error. It didn't count that I, a woman, had pointed it out.

"Yes, we will rent you the car."

In time I was able to acquire a credit card on my own. It came through the bank that held my house mortgage. The bank knew I owned the house and had never failed a payment. They also knew I had reported a bank error *crediting* me with my payment instead of debiting me. Was gratitude why the bank allowed me a credit card? Or was it because the banker was a woman? Either way women's rights were finally beginning to take hold.

* * * *

But not totally, and not where there was autism. 1970s men also controlled female opinion. If they couldn't rule it out, they questioned it. And that unnerved us. We struggled to justify our choices; but with autism there never are any clear-cut choices, and we didn't want to be accused of "wanting to wear the pants." Though today's millennials are coming forward with their "#metoo" stories, they have no idea how shaky we mothers were in the 1970s when women's lib had not yet taken hold, and the reality of autism was still pretty much unknown.

THE *EQUUS* STORY

Though Truffaut's film *The Wild Child* had been released in 1969, I doubt if Truffaut himself knew about autism. And me? Though I'd raised Temple, studied extensively, and should have been able to spot Truffaut's Victor as autistic, I didn't. I had yet to put the picture together. Or even dare to.

In this anxious, culturally bewildered decade, Peter Shaffer's play *Equus* opened in New York City in 1973. It told the tale of an emotionally troubled boy and of the equally troubled psychiatrist who treats him. The boy had stabbed out the eyes of six horses with a metal spike. In his introductory notes, playwright Shaffer tells how he came upon the story.[1] It was a crime, he said, that had shocked local magistrates, but there was no explanation save that the boy was disturbed.

"I knew very strongly that I wanted to interpret it in some entirely personal way. I had to create a mental world in which the deed could be made comprehensible."[2]

I wasn't sure I understood Shaffer's "mental world," yet I found myself in thrall to his play, weeping without knowing why. To quote the play: I and all the rest of us had our *"educated average head...held at the wrong angle."*[3] In order to tamp down the stress it created, we were turning to psychiatry for help while psychiatry itself was *"all reined up in old language and old assumptions."*[4] Shaffer was not merely dramatizing the plight of an autistic boy and psychiatry's attempt to help him. He was dramatizing the effect of autism on us, the so-called normal ones.

1. and 2. *A Note on the Play*, Avon, first Bard Printing, 1975.

3. and 4. Quotes are from *Equus*.

Equus opens with the boy, Alan, embracing the horse Nugget. The chained horse and troubled boy stand together nuzzling in the dark *"like a necking couple."*[5]

Is bestiality a stand-in for homosexual love? Or is Shaffer showing us the deeply satisfying behavior of an autistic boy who doesn't know how to connect to humans yet yearns for the warm touch of a living creature?

I found myself thinking of Temple who didn't want to be touched but desperately needed to hug and be hugged—how she had created her squeeze machine so she could hug herself. I think, too, of the doctor who'd sensed that premature babies needed to be held; how she took them out of their incubators with the life supporting tubes still attached, and laid them in their mothers' arms so each could feel the warmth of the other. Her hope was that

Pittsburgh Public Theater

this would fulfill the infant's need for touch and thereby forestall the autism preemies are at risk of developing. I can't speak for the baby, but I saw what the act meant to the baby's mother: the quiet joy in her face, the way her fingers stroked the baby's cheek.

Shaffer is dramatizing the same humble, ever human need for touch. Maybe for Alan it involves sex, why wouldn't it? The boy's adolescent. But sex is not all that gives the scene

5. Ibid.

with Nugget its meaning. Burdened with the psychic isolation of autism, Alan has found his way to fulfilling this need, and Nugget the horse has responded. The two are now bound together physically and psychically.

The stage goes dark; in the dark, the psychiatrist Dysart strikes a match and lights a cigarette. As a spot comes up on him, he confides to the audience his distraught conflict.

His emotional hunger and his professional commitment to child psychiatry are at odds with each other. He likens Nugget's chained love of the free spirited boy to his own troubled self *"straining to jump clean hoofed on to a whole new track of being I only suspect is there."*

Is playwright Shaffer saying that the belief in psychiatric counseling as a cure for autism is dated, useless and cruel? That meddling with an autistic's joy over connecting with a horse is a killer practice? Dysart goes on to describe seeing himself in a dream where he's become a Sun God priest sacrificing children on a bloody altar.

Nevertheless—holding tight to his psychiatric authority—Dysart continues to question Alan. And Alan, in return, chants advertising jingles at him. Even in the 1970s, I knew Alan's jingles signaled "echolalia," but I didn't see him as autistic; I still had my own *"educated average head...held at the wrong angle."* But when Dysart probes Alan's parents for their role in causing the boy's behavior, I connected instantly to Bruno Bettelheim and his intention when applying for a grant from the Ford Foundation:

"Besides treating his autistic patients, he intended to explore what their parents had done 'wrong' in raising them."[6]

6. Pollock, *The Creation of Dr. B*, page 251.

The play's final scene plays out in the style of a late 1940s drama where the psychiatrist is once again the hero-who-comes-up-with-the-answer-that-puts-everything-right. Except that this psychiatrist has woeful doubts. Trapped in ambiguity, Dysart talks Alan into reenacting the blinding of the horses, and we, identifying with both characters, watch in agony.

Night rides with Nugget have been Alan's unfettered animal joy. It's an ecstasy that's as close he can get to what we call "soul." And Nugget has been his witnessing partner. Since Alan believes God's all-seeing eye witnesses everything, Nugget has become Alan's God. So when Alan has sex with the young girl, when he shares the same ecstasy with her, and Nugget has watched, the only way out of his pain is to blind Nugget and all horses like him. That way no horse will ever again witness Alan's betrayal of his God.

Pittsburgh Public Theater

Alan's agonized solution has an autistic logic to it. I think of an autistic boy who's the same age as Alan and is under medication to relieve his anxiety. One day he decided that if taking one pill could give him a day free of anxiety, then taking the entire bottle of pills would free him forever. He ended up in a hospital emergency.

* * * *

Equus won the 1975 Tony award for best play; and in 1977 was made into a film with real horses instead of actors symbolizing horses. Though the film also won awards, it didn't quite work. Film is literal; the play's power lies in its poetically imagined symbolism.

Nevertheless, the film captured enough of the play's essence for New York Times critic Vincent Canby to call *Equus* "an extraordinarily skillful, passionate inquiry into the entire Freudian method."[7]

Pittsburgh Public Theater

Whew! A theatre authority has noted the crucial question playwright Shaffer has dramatized:

Is the Freudian method the key to autism's social disconnection or are our *"educated average heads"* still turned toward Freudian interpretation for just about everything?

Why hadn't one of us asked that question back in 1943 when Kanner told us that our cold parenting had caused autism? Again when Bettelheim upped the ante? Right then, why hadn't some ordinary soul asked straight-out: what does Freud's search for psychic trauma caused by inappropriate social behavior have to do with children who can't interact socially at all! Could we please take another look at what Freud actually said about his own practice?

According to a well-known, present-day psychoanalyst[8] Freud was reputed to conclude that suffering was the overall human condition: that maybe after years of his psychoanalysis a neurotic might finally make the transition from debilitating neurosis to ordinary human suffering.[9]

7. Wikipedia.

8. and 9. Bernice Hoffman, Ph.D., Clinical Psychologist Psychoanalyst

There's no record that Freud ever worked with children. Nor did Bleuler. Bleuler worked with patients in the Burgholzli hospital in Zurich; and coined the word "autism" to describe those of them who had withdrawn from all social contact. In Bleuler's day, an autistic child would most likely have been labeled "retarded."

ANNA FREUD'S STORY

Anna Freud (Freud's daughter) did work with children. The following quote from her 1943 study *War and Children* (written in tandem with Dorothy Burlingham) reveals direct experience with autistic children and insight into their disconnection:

> *"The opposite of love isn't hate, but egotism. When the emotions are unable go outside of the person."*

Her study, published during WWII, tells how British children were housed in country townships to keep them safe from London bombing; until it became apparent that being separated from their mothers was more traumatizing than living through the London "blitz."

To give us a sense of children and the "blitz," British actress Rosemary Harris, in her New York nightclub act, described how, during the bombing, Londoners took refuge in the underground "tube." When bombs fell, shaking the entire station, mothers rocked their children and sang "There'll be blue birds over the White Cliffs of Dover/Tomorrow when the world is free" We knew the song here in the States, but hadn't realized that it was to comfort children—not till Harris broke our hearts miming rocking a child and singing:

The shepherd will tend his sheep
The valley will bloom again
And Jimmy will go to sleep
In his own little room again
There'll be bluebirds over
The white cliffs of Dover
Tomorrow just you wait and see

Comforting Jimmy with a song was only one side of the story. Jimmy's mother needed Jimmy, needed to hold him in her arms, rocking and singing with the other mothers. Four years earlier in 1939, Anna Freud had negotiated the rescue of her father from Nazi Vienna and brought him to London. Not just for his sake, but for hers.

In times of war, no one is theoretical.

12

THE ASPERGER STORY
1980s–1990s

In the final years of the 1970s, parents of autistic children were aware that some of their offspring were highly intelligent, sometimes exceptionally gifted, but never quite seemed to grow up. Schools were calling them "little professors." Playwright Peter Shaffer appears to have felt a kinship with them. In his published edition of *Equus*, he admits that when he was working in a branch of the New York Public Library, he became convinced that the nature of his thinking made him unemployable. In 1979 he gave us *Amadeus*, a play about Mozart; who in spite of his musical genius remained infuriatingly childish all of his life. Today "Aspies" claim Mozart as one of them.

****

The term "Asperger's"—with its moniker "Aspie"—didn't surface officially until 1981, when Lorna Wing published a paper describing the work of Dr. Hans Asperger, a licensed psychiatric pediatrician practicing at the University of Vienna from the 1940s through the 1960s. (He died in 1980.) Wing's paper gave medical recognition to Asperger's definition of a certain type of autism: bright self-absorbed young with superior reasoning powers who remain undeveloped socially. In 1992, Uta Frith translated Asperger's writings into English: further reinforcing his work and the autism category he defined. Thus the term *Asperger Syndrome* became the accepted medical term for a recognizable type of autism.

But not for long.

In 2013, the American Psychiatric Association released the fifth edition of its *Diagnostic and Statistical Manual of Mental Disorders* (DSM-5) and deleted the term. Any autistic who evidenced the traits known as "Asperger Syndrome" would now ride under the all-inclusive definition: *Autism Spectrum Disorder*. The story why goes something like this.

In 1943, when Dr. Leo Kanner of Johns Hopkins University put autism on the U.S. map, gossip circulated that Kanner had in some way been connected to Hans Asperger in Vienna. But as far as we were concerned, Hans Asperger was just another Viennese pediatrician involved in a German eugenics program that looked pretty much like our own. Both programs had begun in the 1930s, both were medically approved, and both addressed those deemed "unfit to reproduce." In 1943, when the United States was at war with Japan and Germany, we interned the Japanese Americans but not the German Americans. We took this partisan act of discrimination as casually as we would the atomic bombing of the Japanese two years later.

It all looks quite different today. Today we want to know exactly what was going on in Nazi Germany's eugenics program in 1943. Had Hans Asperger—the pediatrician who developed the idea of a childhood psychopathy that existed on a spectrum—been assigned the job of culling the children whom the Nazis saw as "unfit to live," keeping alive those whose ability to systemize might prove useful in breaking wartime codes? Or had the doctor dreamed up a new psychosocial category in order to rescue a handful of children whom he felt resembled his boyhood self?

The question stirs up another question. Yes, Hans Asperger was a Nazi. And yes, we've credited him with defining a recognizable type of autism—in fact, named it after him. But does he deserve the credit? The theory of autism existing on a spectrum was already under competitive development in Austria. How Dr. Asperger *interpreted* the theory in terms of Nazi eugenics is where we need to look. That being so, we better look first at our own role in the history of eugenics.

In 2016, *Harvard Magazine* printed an article by Adam Cohen covering Harvard's participation in American eugenics from the late 1800s through the 1980s. Very decent of Harvard to include this dubious chapter in its history: reason enough to include a synopsis[1] of it here.

Harvard's story starts in the late nineteenth century when the first enthusiasm for eugenics arrived from England in the form of an opinion devised by a half cousin of Darwin: one Francis Galton. After studying the families of some of history's greatest thinkers, Galton had concluded that genius was hereditary. And therefore,

> *"what nature does, blindly slowly and ruthlessly, man may do providentially, quickly and kindly."*[2]

Charles Darwin, if you recall, believed in the high intellectual worth of "a body of well instructed men." The elite of Boston, all well-instructed Harvard men, took to Cousin Galton's notion like ducks to water. Dr. Oliver Wendell Holmes Sr., dean of the Harvard Medical School, rearranged it this way:

---

1. and 2. Synopsis, quotes, and pictures: *Harvard Magazine*, March–April 2016.

"If genius and talent are inherited...why should not deep-rooted moral defects...show themselves...in the descendants of moral monsters?"

Dr. Holmes'question brought forth so many nods of approval that in 1911 Frank Taussig, whose publication on economics was a popular textbook, recommended sterilization in large print:

"The human race would be immensely improved in quality...if those of poor physical and mental endowment were prevented from multiplying."

William Ernest Castle, listed as a Professor of Zoology, opined that race mixing produced inferior offspring. Would that his opinion had stayed in the classroom, but students graduate and develop causes. The eugenics cause joined forces with the immigration quota cause. The two causes agreed that the rapidly arriving "huddled masses" had little to offer the United States in the way of *"physical and mental endowment."*

Providence Evening Bulletin

This led to the 1924 Immigration Act; enacted to keep to a minimum the immigration of Jews, Italians, and Asians. Following suit, Harvard's President A. Lawrence Lowell set a quota on Jewish students and worked to keep Black students from living in the Harvard Yard. It was all part of "keep America strong."

In 1927, the revered Justice Oliver Wendell Holmes, son of Dr. Holmes of the Harvard Medical School, urged the nation *"to get serious about eugenics and prevent large numbers of unfit Americans from reproducing."*[3] His words took on clout with his ruling in the famous case of Buck vs. Bell. Justice Holmes declared of Carrie Buck, her mother and her baby that "three generations of imbeciles are enough." Carrie Buck was not an imbecile, nor was her mother or her baby. She was poor, luckless, and pregnant by a foster family rapist.

In the 1930s, as the Nazis were moving into power, U.S. enthusiasm for sterilization began to wane. But not entirely. In 1942, when WWII was at its peak, the U.S. Supreme Court could have overturned the Buck vs. Bell verdict but did not. In post war 1950,

3. Ibid.

Ernest Hooton, chairman of Harvard's anthropology department, wrote in a *Redbook* article:

"There can be little doubt of the increase during the past 50 years of mental defectives, psychopaths, criminals, economic incompetents and the chronically diseased. We owe this to the intervention of charity, 'welfare' and medical science, and to the reckless breeding of the unfit."[4]

Some states continued to sterilize the unfit until 1981 (the year Lorna Wing gave us the term *Asperger Syndrome*). Though we never went so far as to exterminate people, we deliberately made them less and suffered no legal consequences.

NOTE: The following quote is from a *New York Times* 7/12/2021 interview with a 1980 sterilization victim listed as "feeble minded."

Victim: *That's a very painful thing…that your government allowed this to happen to you. For them to go inside your body at such a young tender age. My body wasn't even developed.*

Though the *Times* said there'd been some state reparation since, our country is still in too shaky a position to pass judgment on German eugenics. Nevertheless, there sits Hans Asperger. His story deserves a closer look.

In her carefully researched book *ASPERGER'S CHILDREN: The Origins of Autism in Nazi Vienna,* Edith Sheffer writes that, very early in the international game, Nazi leaders recognized the tribal power inherent in a cooperative community kinship; and sensed how to manipulate it into an autocracy.[5] Stressing the

4. Ibid.

5. Edith Sheffer, *ASPERGER'S CHILDREN: The Origins of Autism in Nazi Vienna*, Norton & Co, New York, copyright 2018.

word *gemut* (German for "soul"), they imposed a country-wide education system that taught growing children how to think and act cooperatively for the greater glory of the community. From this "community first" spirit grew a "nation first" *gemut* that rapidly transformed into Nazi law.

Despite Nazi law, officials soon found they were faced with a significant number of children who were unable to think and act cooperatively. Vienna's pediatric psychologists diagnosed them as having "defective *gemut*." Doctors prescribed a stay at Spiegelgrund, a clinic specializing in what was termed "rehabilitation." At Spiegelgrund those who couldn't "rehabilitate" were eliminated. (Many did not make past the first interview.) Those who showed cooperative possibilities were held indefinitely and subjected to a daily routine of physical and emotional "discipline." A handful of Spiegelgrund survivors told Sheffer their stories. They take your breath away.

Spiegelgrund kept records and the records still exist. Dr. Hans Asperger played a crucial role.

In her book's acknowledgements, Sheffer credits her son Eric with her dedication and includes his own words about himself. Eric has autism.

Would he have made it past the first interview with Dr. Asperger?

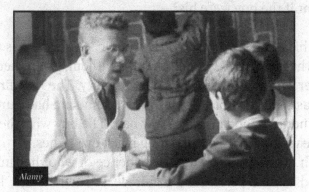
Alamy

In 1961 when I was studying the developmentally impaired, a New England doctor told me I should visit a ward for the seriously malformed. "I'll go with you," he said. "It can be hard to bear. But if you're going to write about those who are less than perfect, they deserve your attention." The ward was closed to the public.

The day we came, the door to the ward *was open*; and sitting by it was an aged Down syndrome woman crooning to a baby with a hydrocephalic head. She held the baby on her shoulder, rocked back and forth hugging the baby, letting its immense head dangle and bobble.

A two-year-old boy stood up in his crib to greet us. His hands gripping the crib railing were raw, pulpy stumps. Born with no sensation of pain, he'd gnawed off the ends of his fingers.

A girl of six, no bigger than a doll, lay flat in her crib. She has no joints. A boy of fourteen sat up in a hospital bed—his head so huge it has to be propped on a pillow, his body the size of a toddler. Yes, the ward was hard to bear, as the doctor said it would be—that life can come into the world this impaired. And survive. I think of Dr. Oliver Wendell Holmes:

"If genius and talent are inherited...why should not deep-rooted moral defects...show themselves...in the descendants of moral monsters?"

What if the boy were his?

In this ward not open to the public, someone has cared for each of these beings—washed them, fed them, given them dignity. I've never forgotten the ward's quiet dignity. The tiny girl with no joints was wearing a plaid doll's dress. Someone had purchased it, dressed her in it, and arranged her hair. The boy with the hydrocephalic head had dark eyes and long black eye lashes.

Each of these children bore evidence of who they might have been had nature dealt them a fair deal. Their hearts, like mine, beat in perfect iambic. Thump *thump*, thump *thump*: the rhythm of Shakespeare's verse.

"We keep them alive for us," the doctor said.

Though the United States eugenics record of is far from ideal and our future record unknown, in 1961 we created a ward where our most severely impaired were welcome.

13

THE MIRROR NEURON STORY
1990s–2018

"Tell me where is fancy bred?
Or in the heart or in the head?
How begot, how nourished?
Reply, reply."

All any of us could reply was that those sudden bursts of sensation Shakespeare in *The Merchant of Venice* called "fancy" weren't begot in the head. But in the heart? How could the heart (essentially a pump) account for moments when we said, "My heart sank" or "My blood ran cold"? Bio-neurologist Antonio Damasio told us we were not thinking beings who feel, we were feeling beings who think; but he couldn't explain how feeling was begot. Nor could the Austrian neurologists account for their "gemut." Despite a post WWII fear that science might lead us back into the dark politics of eugenics, neurologists soldiered on, looking for a clue, any clue. Then in 1996 Giacomo Rizzolati, a neuroscientist at the University of Parma, Italy, stumbled on a neurological connection so astounding that it took him and his colleagues more than a year to believe and verify what they had beheld.[1]

It happened like this:

In Dr. Rizzolati's lab there was a monkey with wires implanted in brain areas that involve planning and carrying out physical movements. It was a hot afternoon in Parma, and the lab technician who took care of the monkey walked into the lab licking an ice cream cone. Suddenly the monkey's wires let out a "brrrr - brrrr"—the sound they make when the monkey himself actually licks the ice cream. The lab technician licked again. Again the wires let out a "brrrr." Though the monkey didn't move, what he was watching had activated the brain area used for planning and carrying out physical movements. There for all the scientific world to see was evidence of a neurological system nobody had ever before witnessed or even imagined! Neurons that imitate the physical action of another being!

The Parma Lab named them "mirror neurons." The internet defined them:

"A mirror neuron is a neuron that fires both when an animal acts and when the animal observes the same action performed by another. Thus, the neuron "mirrors" the behavior of the other, as though the observer were itself acting."[2]

Was this the answer to Shakespeare's riddle? Do humans have these neurons? Dr. Rizzolati said yes.

"Mirror neurons allow us to grasp the minds of others, not through conceptual reasoning but through direct simulation. By feeling not by thinking."[3]

He went on to explain:

1., 2., and 3. *NY Times* – Science 1/10/06.

"The human brain has multiple mirror neuron systems that specialize in carrying out and understanding not just the actions of others but their intentions, the social meaning of their behavior and emotions."[4]

The *Harvard Magazine* (Jan./Feb. 2003) noted:

"...we are just beginning to understand an unexpected new paradigm: certain genes that regulate phenotypes—groups of physiological traits and behaviors—are actually under social control...The environment—even social and cultural contexts—can switch genes on and off." (Hans Hoffman)

It didn't take the everyday world long to figure that mirror neurons could well be the source of empathy: that weird fainting sensation parents feel when rushing a bleeding child to the emergency room while battling their own queasiness. If so, these neurons must have been around for eons, holding us viscerally responsible for each other, drawing us together into families and tribes.

Then, curiously (and despite accumulating evidence), the more socially conservative among us began shrugging off what their disbelieving eyes did not want to behold. Perhaps because, as the *New York Times* science article had predicted in 2006, acceptance of mirror neuron action involved:

"...shifting our understanding of culture, empathy, philosophy, language, imitation, autism and psychotherapy.[5]...Everyday experiences are also being viewed in a new light...how children learn—why people respond to certain types of sports...why watching media violence may be harmful and why many men like pornography."[6]

4., 5., and 6. Ibid.

The social implications of all this stirred up a research finance problem. What major money source would want to fund research that might challenge long upheld belief systems? But it didn't explain why so few autism books were covering the topic. Mirror neurons looked to be playing a major role in social patterning; and social disconnection was a recognized autism problem.

Nearly a generation has passed since that 1/10/06 *Times* article and the controversy it stirred up. The world now accepts the existence of mirror neurons. Scholarpedia defines the system as a mapping device that coordinates "action-understanding, imitation, intention-understanding and empathy."[7]

For "action-understanding" think of learning to tie your shoes. Explanations don't work, someone has to show you. For the other "mapping coordinates" think apprenticeship: how a learned skill is passed from one person to another. I looked for an illustration of "apprenticeship" in my own life and came up with a childhood recollection.

When I was ten, my older cousin (whom I adored and yearned to please) taught me to sail his boat. He showed me how to look for the dark water up ahead. "That's the wind coming," he said. "When you see the dark water hit the bow of the boat, head the into the wind, and we'll go faster." First he did it. I watched and saw how he braced his feet against the gunwale (the top edge of the boat).

"Now you take hold of the tiller."

I imitated how he grabbed the tiller, imitated how he'd braced his feet. My arms felt the pull of the water on the tiller, and I realized that's why he braced his feet. It was lesson number one. Then came lessons two and three: Step by nautical step, the know-how passed from my cousin who "knew the ropes" to me who wanted

7. Ibid.

to learn them. Ever since, when I see a sailboat in a heavy wind, my arms feel again the pull of the water on the tiller—even though, like Rizzolati's monkey, I may not move a muscle.

I think next of how men like to go to ball games. Every boy learns to play baseball. Now he's a man he goes to a ball park (or a bar with TV) to see again, hear again, feel again the "thwak" of a bat hitting the ball; and celebrate the feeling with other men.

My mind roves back to Nicholas the baby asking for a cookie. Do conceptual thinking, context, shared information, and executive function relate to the mirror neuron mapping device that coordinates "action-understanding, imitation, intention-understanding and empathy"?

Nobody yet knows for sure, but it sure looks that way.

"The human brain has multiple mirror neuron systems that specialize in carrying out and understanding not just the actions of others but their intentions, the social meaning of their behavior and emotions." [8]

With Rizzolati swimming in my head, I return to Eric Kandel's 2006 book *In Search of Memory* and fill out the quote excerpted in chapter 3: the section where Kandel introduces Rizzolati and writes that mirror neurons could:

"provide the first insight into imitation, identification, empathy, and possibly the ability to mime vocalization—the mental processes intrinsic to human interaction." [9]

For the seeing/hearing world, the mirror neuron system works primarily with sight and sound. For the blind, there is only sound.

8. www.scholarpedia.org/article/Mirror_neurons
9. *In Search of Memory*, 2006.

Blind Tom's first introduction to music was hearing the Bethune girls sing. He mimicked them and harmonized just as he had already mimed the various hisses and clatters of a railway train. When the Bethune family bought a piano and he heard it played; he sat down and "mirrored" what he had heard, note for note.

Here's an animal reaction that may be due to mirror neurons. I have a friend who plays the accordion; every time she plays, her dog howls.

Kandel gives credence to all such possibilities; then adds his own. Here's the wind-up to his Chapter Three.

> *"In looking at just these three research strands, one can see a whole new area of biology opening up, one that can give us a sense of what makes us social, communicating beings. An ambitious undertaking of this sort might not only discern the factors that enable members of a cohesive group to recognize one another but also teach us something about the factors that give rise to tribalism, which is so often associated with fear, hatred, and intolerance of outsiders."*[10]

All of you bio-neurological heavyweights, please consider undertaking Kandel's suggested research. And while you're at it, give Rizzolati's monkey an ice cream cone. He sure earned it!

* * * *

On July 7, 2021, *The New York Times* Science printed an "Observatory" about Australian cockatoos that raid trash cans in suburban Sydney. Though the trash can lids are tight, the cockatoos are showing each other how to pry them up with their beak and push them off. The act involves three steps. Step one: the cockatoo has to catch the edge of the lid in its beak. Step two: holding onto

10. Ibid.

it (beak-style) it has to walk around the bin rim until the lid is entirely loose. Step three: the bird nudges the lid up and steps into the bin.

What amazed the ecologists was how this three-step maneuver had spread bird to bird, district to district—each bird miming the bird that can do it. The skill didn't turn up "in random locations as it might if different birds had figured out the trash bin technique on their own." It was spreading as human innovation spreads. [11]

Interesting that the ecologist likens the spread to "human innovation" rather than mirror neurons. To quote Ramachandran:

"...A complex skill initially acquired through trial and error... could be transmitted rapidly to every member of a tribe...and in case you haven't guessed by now that ability might hinge on a sophisticated mirror-neuron system." [12]

Accepting mirror neuron action and its effect on both birds and humans may ride on how one reacts socially. If the facts offend, it's easier to refer to "human innovation" than to a neural response we share with the cockatoos. Nevertheless, we do share it, and it points to urges we may not want to face. The cockatoo trick has no long-term social value. It was instant single-minded greed. Garbage. Yet the same mirror neuron response also gave the cockatoos a valuable lifetime skill. Flight. Nature does not judge.

I remember watching a mother blue jay teach her chicks how to fly. The lesson involved wing growth and pluck. The reward: a lifetime of flying.

First the mother jay spread her wings and flew to a nearby telephone wire. Swinging on it, she screamed at her chicks. The

11. James Gorman, NY *Times* Science 7/7/21.

12. *The Tell Tale Brain*, Ramachandran p.132.

first chick teetered on the edge of the nest, spread its wings (as the mother had spread hers), hoisted its fat body into the air, flapped across to the telephone wire, and clung there, terrified. The mother jay screamed at the second chick, and it made the same wobbly journey. Then the next chick, till all four chicks were perched on the telephone wire. The mother jay then flew back to the nest and hollered again. One by one the chicks flapped back; his time with not so much wobble. The process was turning into magic, and the magic was getting to be worth the scare. The next day the nest was empty. Crucial: the jay chicks wanted to fly.

And humans? How do we fit into this?

I think of an afternoon following a social gathering. Most of the crowd had gone home, but a few of us were still sitting around a table, eating the last of the cookies and gossiping. One mother held a nine month baby in her lap. As he munched on his cookie, he stared at each of us as we spoke. Then after a bit he went "Ahhhhhh." He was miming our chat. The reward. A lifetime of talk.

Crucial: The baby wanted to talk.

What about autistic kids who don't want to talk? Or maybe can't?

At a recent family festival there was a karaoke machine, and the kids were all singing into it. After a bit, a five-year-old autistic boy who'd never uttered a sound grabbed the karaoke mic and went "Ahhhhhhhh."

For the first time in his life—the rhythm, the energy, the karaoke mic—it all mattered. It was magic and he wanted to be part of it. The reward: Singing "Ahhhhhhhh" like the other kids.

Ramachandran (whose chapter on autism is valuable reading) believes that *"the main cause of autism is a disturbed mirror neuron system."*[13]

Is the system disturbed? Or maybe just delayed—capable of connecting when the right magic comes along?

"Autism reminds us that the uniquely human sense of self is not an 'airy nothing' without "habitation and a name." Despite its vehement tendency to assert its privacy and independence the self actually emerges from reciprocity of interacts with others."[14]

13. and 14. *The Tell Tale Brain*, Ramachandran.

14

PUTTING IT ALL TOGETHER AND ACTING ON IT

When my children were growing up we lived in a small town about a half hour from Boston. Across the road from us was a farm; on the farm was a henhouse, and in the henhouse lived a rooster. Night after night I'd hear the rooster crow at 3 AM After a stretch I realized that's "first cock crow." The hour when the old day departs and the new day begins is not sunrise, but in the dark of 3 AM Shakespeare tells us that ghosts appear at midnight and depart at "first cock crow." Ghosts belong to what has already happened; the rooster crows for what is about to happen. Though he doesn't know yet what the day will bring, he invites it to start.

All this is a roundabout way to introduce some of the questions families have asked me and some of the scenes we've shared; but bear in mind that the choices we made then belong to what has already happened. Whether they apply to today is open to question. Today New York is battling coronavirus. I look out my Upper West Side window and all I can see on the usually crowded sidewalk is a scattering of people walking six feet apart. By the time you read what I've written, I hope COVID-19 will be history. But since history repeats, it's a good idea to take note of past questions and options.

What was it like to raise Temple before there were Special Ed laws?

You're right; there were no "Special Ed" laws then. What we did have was a network of gifted teachers who were experts at helping children with disability challenges. The teachers all knew each other and knew each other's skills. Each one who guided and supported Temple also guided and supported me. Each one passed the two of us on to the next teacher. It was shared expertise and shared concern.

How has the scene changed?

There are valuable changes, not the least being the social acceptance of autism. But there are also changes that need to be rethought; in particular, the over-professionalizing of autism. Rather than having trained therapists doing all the teaching, I would suggest helping parents learn how to be co-therapists for their children. It reaches back to Eric Schopler's TEACCH. It's how Temple's teachers taught me.

Can you describe this in detail?

Basically, it's a combination of daily one-on-one counseling and coaching. Here's a recollection of how a wise counselor put it to me:

"I've never forgotten my first therapy session with a young mother. Impatient with her lack of skill, I took over, and what I did for her child was instantly better than what she was doing. I thought she'd be grateful, but no; she burst into tears. It took time for me to realize that my skill had made her feel inadequate. I decided then and there that my role *would be to coach. That's hard when you can see how to help—and it's also quicker to do it yourself than to explain what you're doing. But if you do that, you make her feel she'll never be a good mother. It's slower to coach, but in the end it's deeper and more effective."*

Would that all young mothers could have her for a coach.

How does Dad fit into this picture?

Far better than he used to. I think of a Canadian dad; he and his wife were troubled over their child's exhaustion from daily four hour therapy sessions. Dad had found his own way to show his four-year-old how he should behave:

"He loves to get tickled. When he gets it right, I tickle him, and we laugh and hug."

Though Dads are much better at understanding and coping than they used to be, many are still unstrung by autism. Male distress works differently from female distress. For starters, look at the body difference. Women are built to incubate life and make it grow. Our bodies swell with pregnancy, and return to their old shape. We're flexible; we accept life in whatever form it arrives. Men's bodies are muscular and hard to the touch; they're built to fix what is out of order and hold fast to their honorable intent. Autism cannot be fixed in the way that a broken arm can be fixed. So when it arrives, it's liable to swerve into that honorable intent, leaving great black skid marks of shame.

Culture plays a role in that sense of shame. I think of a Latino dad who'd brought his autistic son with him to the autism conference. In the middle of the conference the boy had an epileptic seizure. Afterwards, when the dad talked to me, he relived that agonizing moment. He wanted so much to be a good dad, but humiliation was pressing hard on his Latin pride.

Another conference, this time in Sacramento, California:

After the room emptied, an Asian father and I watched his autistic son climb obsessively over and under every vacant chair in the auditorium. In many Asian cultures, the eldest son is raised to understand that he will be responsible for the care of his elderly parents. High stock is given to honor. The Asian father knew that I knew this and came straight to the point. "What do we do if we can't stand it?"

Do Family Enrichment Weekends help?

The ones I attended certainly did. Families rose above individual problems and bonded with each other into a weekend community.

I think of a police officer at a family weekend. When his autistic son got a driver's license, he'd decided to get a degree in psychology so he could teach other police officers how to recognize the difference between a kid trying to talk his way out of a traffic violation and a kid with autism. He showed the officers how to escort the autistic kid to the station without stirring up anxiety and help him call his parents.

"And, dads, you better get down there quick," says Mac Bledsoe, a cowboy-booted school coach and author of *Parenting with Dignity*. He's talking to a bunch of Nez Perce Indians at a Family Enrichment Weekend in Idaho: big, bulky men, squeezed into metal folding chairs, arms crossed on their chests, and a braid down every back. Their unreadable faces don't scare Bledsoe; he's had a lot of practice grabbing Idaho wheat farmers who are shy when it comes to feelings. Bledsoe gets right to the point with a straight talk on picking up your son at the police station for whatever infraction of the law he's been hauled in for.

"And, Dad, you get down there fast. It doesn't matter if you're wearing a dirty T-shirt."

"Yeah, that's you, Fred," someone cracks.

"It doesn't matter what kind of feeling there's been between the two of you," says Bledsoe. "You just say, 'Son, I don't care what's the right or the wrong of this, we'll figure that out later. Right now we're walking out of here together, a solid front.'"

The men are oddly still. Their autistic sons have been driving tractors since they were big enough to peer over a steering wheel. That doesn't mean they understand—or will ever understand—what a traffic light is for or what a red-light signals.

I look at these men and figure that one of them (maybe Fred) is likely to get a phone call from the cops and will be at the station in a flash. Without a flicker of expression, he'll sling a sturdy arm around his son and walk him home.

In an eastern seaboard culture, male honor operates somewhat differently. There, a dad with an autistic son can get trapped between acceptance and denial unless he bonds with other dads from his own culture. At a Maryland family enrichment conference, I met a sophisticated hotel manager and his beautiful wife. Though the autism conference was at his hotel, he had trouble facing the growing need for him to shoulder the male side of caring for his autistic son. Nevertheless, he attended the presentations and found himself responding to the other men in a wordless sharing. After the conference was over, he invited two of us to lunch with him and his wife. Freed from having to present a brave front she didn't feel, his wife talked openly. The manager sat across from her, looked at this beautiful woman whom he clearly adored, and finally took in the depths of her struggle. Yet I could see the question looming up in him. Can he bear to have his sophisticated lifestyle change? My guess is he can and will. Without being aware of it, he had already bonded with the other men at the conference—as men have always bonded over a ballgame and a beer. Whatever the culture, mirror neurons make the whole world kin.

What about siblings?

Ah, that's a hard one. Siblings are more aware than we realize. They're trying hard to be good little helpers, obedient to the family pattern, so they hide their side of the story because they know it will upset the family dynamic.

Try to arrange a time when you're alone with your helper-sibling child. Nothing amazing, just a shared activity like: "Let's the two of us get dinner tonight—everybody else out of the kitchen." One mother told me, "Oh, the two of us; we go out and get our toenails painted."

At crucial times, a counselor can be invaluable. A child will tell a counselor what they won't tell parents. Also, a very young child may not have the words to explain what's troubling. I think of a wonderful counselor who had a big dollhouse and every sort of figure and furniture you can think of. "I tell them you can decorate the rooms," she said. "The scenes they put together tell me what they're struggling with." The counselor also described making a little tent out of blankets for the child to creep into and a flashlight to light it. "After the child is in there I ask if I may come in." Together in that safe cave, the counselor helps the child understand that she doesn't have to be autism's little helper. She has a right to her own sense of self.

Once that's established, siblings can develop a resilience and empathy that will carry them through childhood and into adult life. Also laughter. As adults they will be quick to recognize when a situation is out-of-proportion absurd. There are plenty of those in the everyday world. Again, remember I write from the past. New teaching techniques keep developing.

At present, are we in an autism epidemic?

We've always had autism. For years we saw autistic children simply as odd and confused their oddity with intellectual impairment. In 1949, when Temple was diagnosed as autistic, the statistic for autism was one in a thousand. Though Temple was odd, it was clear—even in the 50s—that she was not impaired intellectually. For other children it was not that clear. For them there were confused diagnoses: "dyslexia," "attention deficit," "hyperactivity," and "stubborn child." Today's bio-neurological knowledge has contributed to more precise diagnoses. Because of it, autism appears to be on the rise. Also upping the statistic are children whose families have sought out an autism diagnosis in order to apply for government education assistance. All things considered; I do not think we are in an epidemic.

Can measles inoculations cause autism?

According to reliable scientific research, there is no evidence that measles (MMR) inoculations can cause autism. Yet parents continue to believe they do. I suspect that the persistence of their belief comes under the category of easy pop-justified solutions for complex problems. Remember how Leo Kanner said that "refrigerator mothers" caused autism? How Bettelheim took it a step further? For years we believed them both.

Does culture play into autism?

Ah, there it is again: the role that culture plays in our social reactions. Though we like to think of ourselves as independent, we are tribal creatures. Young adults create free-form tribes around whatever power group is in style. CEOs and socialites form discreet tribes with unspoken codes only they can recognize. Longstanding religious groups such as Amish, Mennonite, or Hasidic have faith codes, and shun any tribal member who cannot behave as their code demands. Where there's autism, those demands can present an unresolvable problem.

I think of a bonneted mother (Amish? Mennonite?) who had gained permission to attend an autism conference. She needed help with her autistic child. Behind her stood three bonneted women, their faces stern, their arms tightly folded across their chests. Were they guarding her? Protecting her from information that might violate the tribal code? I felt for that bonneted mother. She'd come so far—risked her own safety. And now what? Should she submit to the laws of her tribe and watch her child slip into autistic isolation? Or break with the tribe and go. Go where?

I never knew what happened. I said my say and the three bonneted women walked her off.

How does our present internet culture affect autism?

In 1969, electronics achieved its first internet connection, and ever since it's been growing like kudzu. Millennials know no other world; and to the consternation of parents, autistic kids love it more than real life. Their choice is understandable. The real world makes them feel awkward and dumb; the internet world makes them feel smart and savvy. Nevertheless, it's a lonely choice— one that separates them from real life and can lead to depression.

"...there are studies that show depression in adolescents to be associated with high amounts of media use, media multitasking, and social media use...We're forgetting the emotional side of active learning." (Sociologist Sherry Turkle. *Harvard Magazine* Nov/Dec 2013)

The internet can also lead to an over sedentary lifestyle. Many autistics and Aspies have low muscle tone; it gives them little urge to get up from their desk, stretch, and go for a walk. They'd rather play games on the computer and eat potato chips.

Here's a worldlier caveat:

Devised first for the internet is an interactive voice system that responds to spoken questions. It often answers in a soft "motherly" voice, and if you are a four-year-old, there's every reason to believe and trust that voice. Like your real mother, it must be telling you the truth. Regretfully, an interactive voice system can be programmed to persuade a four-year-old to want something that can be bought and guide her to a sales website. One mother, realizing how it was undermining her authority, took the device away from her four-year-old. (*NY Times* 10/8/2017)

If children can respond to a computer voice as if it were human, what is its effect on autistic children? Other than inducing isolation, nobody has fully explored the question. Yet more than anything, our autistic young long to join us.

What can you add to the picture of genetics?

Genetics play a major neurological role; and here's a setup where genetically inherited skills play a social role. Systemizing techies who design the internet connections earn far more than do empathizing artists. That makes them top money-making marriage partners. Since like attracts like, techies tend to marry techies; genetically that doubles the systemizing trait. As too much empathy can feed into depression, over systemizing can veer into autism. In Silicon Valley, a noticeably high number of the affluent techies who drove me around in their Jaguars had autistic offspring.

Here's genetic information older men may wish they hadn't been told.

"A woman is born with all the eggs she'll ever carry. By the time a man turns 40, on the other hand, his gonad cells will have divided 610 times to make spermatazoa. By the time he's in his 50s that number goes up to 840. Each time those cells copy themselves; mistakes may appear in the DNA chain. Some researchers now think that a percentage of these mistakes reflects not just random mutations but experienced-based epigenetic markings that insinuate themselves from sperm to fetus and influence brain development. Another theory holds that aging gonad cells are more error prone because parts of the DNA that should have spotted and repaired any mistakes have been epigenetically tamped down. In any case we now know that the children of older fathers show more signs of schizophrenia, autism and bi-polar disorder than children of younger ones." (Judith Shulevitz, Science Editor of *The New Republic*, NY TIMES 9/9/12)

Why so many stories about men?

Because autism is predominately male. The last time I read statistics (and counted the actual number in a classroom) autism tended to be 3-to-1 male; Asperger to be 10-to-1 male. Autistic girls are usually more social than autistic boys. Even as a very young child, Temple wanted to play with the other children. That's not always true of autistic boys; they're more apt to withdraw into their own particular world.

Temple was educated privately.
What about public education?

Though special education, both public and private, has become dependent on systemized instruction, systems can be at odds with the natural flow of growing up. A certain amount of specially designed help can be invaluable, but equally important are general classes with other children. Otherwise, how will an autistic child learn as Temple did, "I have to play the games by the other kids' rules, or they won't let me play with them"? And the other kids, how will they learn what a bright odd duck can bring to their games? Ingenious stuff like Temple's bicycle kites.

Hopefully professionally arranged classes have changed since writing this. More and more schools are recognizing that education is not a systemized science. Teaching (particularly in middle school) rides on insight garnered from years of experience, intuition, and an empathetic willingness to go the imaginative mile.

When I recounted this to a graduating class of Special Education teachers, a senior, already struggling with a difficult autistic boy, raised his hand. "I understand what you're telling me," he said. "But how do I go that imaginative mile?"

"Be his friend."

Today I find myself assembling stories I might have told that senior. Stories like this one from a Catholic family in New York:

Their autistic son so adored the church (the ritual, the costume) that more than anything he wanted to be an altar boy. So the local priest assigned him vestments and trained him in the role. It was a perfect match. Until one Sunday morning when the boy saw another boy, also trained, also wearing vestments, serving the priest. He rose from the family pew, stalked up the aisle and the steps to the altar, swung through the door to where the vestments hung, put on his vestments, and came forth to serve the priest. The priest, without missing a beat, included both boys in the ceremony.

Here's a yarn from a private, pre-K through third grade school in Winston Salem, North Carolina. This little school for autistic four-year-olds came up with a new tuition plan: any neurotypical kindergartener who wanted to attend could come for free. Families already paying for their autistic four-year-old promptly enrolled the siblings; and the siblings, familiar with autism, knew how to play with other autistic four-year-old's, I watched as the nimble showed the less nimble how to do relay races, a game that requires social coordination. A year later I was pleased to learn that the school had a waiting list of neurotypical young who also wanted to attend.

Another memory assembles itself: it's of a public middle-school class in Yakima, Washington. One of the grades included an autistic boy who had a shadow. (A shadow is a trained attendant who "shadows" an autistic student through his classes, prompting him on how to behave.) The class told the shadow "Forget it. Go home, we'll do it." How they worked it out, who knows. Children have their own rules for fair play. All I know is the autistic boy loved it and so did the class.

And still another memory: this one is of an eighth-grade class presentation at an autism conference in Vancouver, Canada. There must have been twenty of them, including one seriously autistic boy. Each classmate gave a brief talk on understanding autism. The class also featured one of them playing a piano solo. During the solo—to everyone's surprise—the autistic boy responded to the piano music, hopped up on the stage, and began a wild dance. The class teacher hopped up after him, danced a turn or two with him, and danced him off. The soloist was happy, the autistic boy was happy, and the audience was captivated by the teacher's friendly solution.

As her class lined up for pictures, I thought one of those twenty kids will have a child on the autism spectrum and it won't be a big deal.

One last memory: all those years ago when Temple was a third-grader at Dedham Country Day School, her teacher and I agreed that if Temple was having a bad day I would come and take her home. The teacher used those days to explain autism to the class. Now that they're all of them in their 70's, they feel they had a hand in helping their friend Temple achieve her PhD and become famous.

What about those who are not up to Temple's level?

That's an important question; I'm glad you brought it up. Though we're good at recognizing different levels of capability and finding a suitable job for each of them, there are still those who confound us. We know how to allow for the big glitches, but what about the small unhappy ones? Like the time it can take a young autistic to figure out a green traffic light, pull himself together, and get across the street before it turns red? Because we do it without thinking, we forget how hard it is for those who can't generalize. We also forget that when he's making his way across the street, that young autistic is also battling eczema and sensitivity to street noise. If this brief task takes such a toll, a day-long job full of interruption and office noise may not be possible. In truth, no job may be possible. The best this young man may be able to achieve is daily dignified survival.

We need to shine a gentler light on such young, remembering that autism comes in all varieties: some bright, some less so, some with well-coordinated bodies, some hampered by low muscle tone and limited dexterity. We also need to remember that autistic teenagers can go through sudden emotional upheavals—one moment able to cope, the next totally out of it.

I remember a severely autistic sixteen-year-old who'd made a name for himself teaching cops how to recognize autism. One day he got upset, escaped his mother (it was easy, he's twice her size) dodged between speeding cars to his favorite vacant lot where he flung himself down and wept like a baby. His mother, frantic, called 911. The cops found him and were startled to realize that this sobbing, incoherent boy was the same poised young man who had instructed them on autism. His mother called me in despair.

"If this is teenage autism, how will I survive?"

Don't despair, desperate mother. You say your boy is scheduled for "assisted living" and "assisted living" means just what the words say. When Temple was a teenager and having a rough time of it, she went to an assisted-living high school that was also a farm. She loved farm life, loved riding the horses, feeding them, caring for them. It's how her focus on animal behavior began. And look where it has taken her: top professor on animal behavior at Colorado State University. Above and beyond her professional success, I treasure how Temple and I talk to each other these days. Her visceral response to the pain a cow suffers from an injured hoof has opened her up to understanding human distress.

Right now, you and your boy feel overwhelmed, but to your surprise people will respond and help you more than you think they will—as the cops helped find your boy. The cops knew him from his autism talks, so it mattered to them to find him. Now they know him in a deeper more complicated way and will do everything they can to lessen the load for you both. We're like ducks flying in a V. The lead duck takes the brunt of the wind. Then after a stretch, another duck takes over so the lead duck can rest in the back wind. Webster calls this "altruism" and defines it as "regard for, and devotion to, the interests of others."

* * * *

In the early 1950s—not yet ten years after WWII—we were in Paris when my father's brother, Austin Purves, a well known artist, was constructing a war memorial he'd designed for a chapel in southern France. The French wanted to honor the 861 American soldiers who were killed in "Operation Dragoon" and are buried in a cemetery in Draguignan. The memorial, a mosaic, was to be a Pietà: the Madonna holding a dead G.I. in Her arms.

In an atelier in Paris my uncle and his assistants were assembling the mosaic from a maquette. They'd laid sheets of brown paper on the floor and were gluing the individual pieces onto them right side down. When completed, the sheets would be shipped to Draguignan, cemented to the chapel wall, the brown paper stripped away, and voila: the Pietà right side up.

"What if you've made a mistake?" I asked.

"It happens all the time" my uncle said. "You get out a pickaxe; then re-assemble and re-cement."

Human behavior can go awry far more easily than a misarranged mosaic; only you can't take a pickaxe to it and re-assemble. Recognizing our flawed humanity, the artists of Notre Dame adorned their most holy of holies with gargoyles, thereby acknowledging and pardoning the less holy side of human nature.

It was Holy Week that week in Paris; Notre Dame had announced it would present a Passion Play that evening. Despite a drizzling rain, we followed the locals to where a platform had been erected in front of Notre Dame, and a path cleared leading up to it. The crowd assembled on each side of the path and waited. At the appointed hour, we saw stumbling toward us a naked man in a loin cloth, half-lugging, half-dragging two crudely nailed wooden beams. The man's head was bowed under their weight—so close to us we could see him pulling the longer beam free each time it caught in the pavement cracks under our feet. When the man finally reached the platform, Roman helmeted guards grabbed him, and before we thought it could happen, they'd hauled the beams upright and had nailed the man's hands to the shorter piece. A rough device for torture and death was suddenly transformed into a crucifix.

At that, the "mouth of hell" lit up on the platform and out of it sprang demons holding Judas Iscariot aloft like a trophy, bearing him back down again to burn forever in the fiery pit. Now the devil himself emerged from the pit and danced in triumph in front of Notre Dame.

Suddenly, abruptly, the devil, the demons, and the mouth of hell vanished. High in the cathedral arches shone a spot—and with it a burst of trumpet. Haloed in sound and light was the angel Gabriel.

The crowd looked up transfixed. All that Notre Dame had celebrated for 600 years was in that redeeming image. Then slowly, very slowly, the image faded. Awe leached from the crowd, and Paris took itself home.

For Paris, the miracle. For those with autism, maybe not. The performance was a mix of reality and symbolism with no demarcation between the two. A very real man lugged two very real boards along a path so narrow that any one of us could have reached out and touched his rain-soaked back. Nailing him to the boards looked real, but then—without warning—the man and the boards turned into a symbol. How is an autistic child to know which is which? The question so haunted me that I began to imagine a story.

Remember the boy who wanted to know why I, the autism authority, would do such a dumb thing as vacuum my basement? Because the boy's question continued to haunt me, I found myself dreaming up what might have happened if he and I had come to the Passion play together. I see the two of us standing amid a crowd enthralled with a performance that looks to the boy as dumb as vacuuming a basement. Yet he senses there's something going on that he might understand, perhaps even take part, if I could just explain it to him.

And I can't.

But knowing how he wants the world to make sense, I quote him the words of neuroscientist Antonio Damasio:

"At their best, feelings point us in the proper direction, take us to the appropriate place in a decision-making space, where we may put the instruments of logic to good use."

He likes the quote; it comforts his logic seeking soul. But it doesn't comfort me. My feelings are not looking for a decision making space; they're responding to my mirror neurons. So now I quote him the words of neuroscientist Giacomo Rizzolati:

"Mirror neurons allow us to grasp the minds of others, not through conceptual reasoning but through direct simulation. By feeling not by thinking."

But "direct simulation" doesn't cut it either. Maybe there's a better Rizzolati quote? Both of us need more.

"The human brain has multiple mirror neuron systems that specialize in carrying out and understanding not just the actions of others but their intentions, the social meaning of their behavior and emotions."

"Intentions," that's more like it; but what about our misguided intentions? How do we confront them? Get over them? Forgive each other for them?

I grab the boy's arm:

"Come. Let's go see what the gargoyles have to say."

"Gargoyles?"

"Notre Dame has more than one story to tell."

The gargoyles of Notre Dame are fantastic creatures serving a practical intention. It's their job, I tell the boy, to sit out on the cathedral towers and catch the rainwater before it sluices down the side of the building damaging the stonework. They're rain spouts.

Alamy

They also serve a meaningful intention: they are there to remind us that we're far from perfect. Maybe like them: a little grotesque. They stand for all the fantastic errors we create for ourselves, and will go on creating. The big difference between us and the gargoyles is that the gargoyles can't change. We can. And over time we do.

* * * *

Long ago when those creatures were first erected, the crowd attending a Notre Dame Passion Play would have been much like the crowd we've been standing among tonight—yet with a major historic difference: The crowd would have called you a witch child, a "changeling," and burned you up. Since witchcraft was a legal felony with death by burning, it would have been logical to burn a changeling. Logic without feeling can create monsters.

Then in 1799, the artist Goya depicted the sleep of reason—how it can create monsters. The truth is: we need both reason and feeling if we want to think with wisdom.

Over the years we've tried to do just that, and on the whole life has improved for those of you with autism. Yet even with good intention and scientific know-how, wisdom can escape us. Like the gargoyles. We're a bit grotesque. But then, so is autism. You kids are not easy.

Part of the problem is that nobody wants to say any of this out loud. So it all gets hidden and you and I have a lot more trouble than we ought to have.

We say to the schools: "Make these children act like us."

And when that doesn't work the way we think it ought to work, we say to genetic research: "Make these children be like us."

At a recent autism conference, I told the story of how Temple was expelled from school by the headmaster who called her "a menace to society." During the Q&A, a little girl came forward. She couldn't have been more than eight; her mother was with her.

"I'm autistic," she said. "Why didn't the teacher like me?"

The room was suddenly still.

Another conference: this time a medical researcher told the story of the advances in genetic research. During the Q&A, a young man spoke up.

"I'm Asperger," he said. "Is the point of your research to do away with me?"

Again the room was still.

* * * *

There is no mission statement for autism. I've taken my cue from the complicated, insightful James Joyce—rambled through the world's stream-of-autism-consciousness, only to find that it's circled me back to the beginning, as Joyce found the river Liffey brought him "by a commodious vicus of recirculation back to Howth Castle and Environs."

Only the Environs aren't the same anymore. The changelings have turned into real people asking us questions we have yet to answer.

I, too, am not the same. Following the trail of autism's confused reaction to us has revealed our confused reaction to autism.

It's up to you now. I turn the story over to you. No answers, just choices. Chopped markings on trees blazing another trail.

THE END

ACKNOWLEDGMENTS

Grateful thanks go to my family, who've been generous and supportive throughout the long process of writing this book. Extra thanks go to my son, Richard Grandin, who has dealt daily with my computer incompetence.

Top thanks go to Chris Curry, autism consultant and close friend. She read my rambles, assumed the role of critic and conscience, and contributed her professional know-how on coping with schooling and on legal protection of autistics.

Editing thanks go to Michael Denneny, New York freelance editor. His advice on organizing topics and his spotting where I rambled off track have been a boon. "It's not that rambles are irrelevant," he said. "It's that they pull the reader's attention off the line of thought you want them to follow."

For information and insight into autism, I'm deeply grateful to Uta Frith, Professor of Cognitive Development, and Tony Attwood, British psychologist noted for guiding Asperger teenagers suffering from depression. I treasure the times I've been with them.

Gratitude also goes to Dr. Raun Melmed in Arizona, Ruth Sullivan (now, alas, deceased) in West Virginia, Catherine Lord in Los Angeles, Joseph Buxbaum in New York, and Gary Mesibov in North Carolina. All of them are pioneers in the autism field. Special thanks go to Richard Pollak, novelist, journalist, and friend, for allowing me unlimited use of quotes from his biography of Bruno Bettelheim: *The Creation of Dr. B*, a valuable source of autism history.

When it comes to the complicated task of publishing *Autism and Us*, Future Horizons deserves top accolades.

SELECTED BIBLIOGRAPHY

Campbell, Joseph. *The Masks of God: Creative Mythology*. New York: Viking Press; first edition (January 1, 1968)

Campbell, Joseph. *The Masks of God: Primitive Mythology*. San Francisco: New World Library; illustrated edition (December 29, 2020)

Clark, Kenneth. *Civilization: A Personal View*. London: British Broadcasting Corporation and John Murray; first edition (January 1, 1969)

Damasio, Antonio R. *Descartes Error: Emotion, Reason and the Human Brain*. New York: Penguin Books; illustrated edition (September 27, 2005)

Damasio, Antonio R. *Looking for Spinoza: Joy, Sorrow, and the Feeling Brain*. Boston: Mariner Books; first edition (December 1, 2003)

Damrosch, Leo. *The Club: Johnson, Boswell, and the Friends Who Shared an Age*. New Haven: Yale University Press; illustrated edition (January 14, 2020)

Dickens, Charles. *Our Mutual Friend: The Allure and Peril of Money*. New York: Penguin Classics; illustrated edition (February 01, 1998)

Dickens, Charles. *The Life and Adventures of Nicholas Nickleby*. New York: Penguin Classics; Penguin Classics edition (November 1, 1999)

Douglas, Ann. *Terrible Honesty: Mongrel Manhattan in the 1920s*. New York: Farrar, Straus and Giroux; reprint edition (January 31, 1996)

Eiseley, Loren. *The Immense Journey: An Imaginative Naturalist Explores the Mysteries of Man And Nature*. New York: Vintage (January 12, 1959)

Frith, Uta. *Autism: Explaining the Enigma*. Hoboken: Wiley-Blackwell; second edition (April 18, 2003).

Groopman, Jerome. *Anatomy of Hope: How People Prevail in the Face of Illness*. Manhattan: Random House Trade Paperbacks; reprint edition (January 11, 2005)

Groopman, Jerome. *How Doctors Think: Analyzing Mistakes Made in Diagnosis and Treatment*. Boston: Mariner Books; reprint edition (March 12, 2008)

Kandel, Eric R. *In Search of Memory: The Emergence of a New Science of Mind*. New York: W. W. Norton & Company; illustrated edition (March 17, 2007)

Melville, Herman. *Bartleby The Scrivener*. Brooklyn & London: Melville House (May 01, 2004)

Melville, Herman. *Billy Budd, Sailor*. Brooklyn & London: Melville House (Dec 06, 2016)

Pollak, Richard. *The Creation of Dr. B: A Biography of Bruno Bettelheim.* Portland: BookBaby; first edition (January 1, 1997)

Ramachandran. V.R. *The Tell-Tale Brain: A Neuroscientist's Quest for What Makes Us Human.* New York: W. W. Norton & Company; reprint edition (January 23, 2012)

Scull, Andrew. *Hysteria: The Disturbing History.* Oxford University Press, USA; illustrated edition (January 1, 2012)

Sheffer, Edith. *Asperger's Children: The Origins of Autism in Nazi Vienna.* New York: W. W. Norton & Company; reprint edition (March 10, 2020)

Showalter, Elaine. *The Female Malady: Women, Madness and English Culture, 1839–1980.* Oxford: University Press, USA; illustrated edition (January 1, 2012)

Snow, C.P. *The Two Cultures and The Scientific Revolution.* Eastford, Conn: Martino Fine Books (December 11, 2013)

AUTHOR BIOGRAPHY

 Eustacia Cutler, author and renowned speaker on autism, brings to national and international conferences her extensive research and personal insight into the nature of autism and the confusion it creates for both child and family, whatever the country.

She earned a B.A. from Harvard, was a band singer at New York's Pierre Hotel, composed and performed cabaret acts, and wrote school lessons for major TV networks. Her research on autism and the developmentally disabled laid the groundwork for two WGBH documentaries: *The Disquieted* on autism; and *The Innocents*, a prize winning first on the developmentally impaired.

Her 2006 book, *A Thorn in My Pocket*, describes raising her daughter Temple Grandin in the 1950s when autistic children were diagnosed as infant schizophrenics and banished to institutions. Today Temple Grandin, Ph.D. is a top professor of animal science and the world's most revered autistic.

Mother and daughter have founded the Temple Grandin and Eustacia Cutler Autism Fund, a nonprofit organization that provides education and support for families with autism and the latest medical information for professionals. Webinars with Eustacia Cutler and other experts can be found at www.templegrandineustaciacutlerautismfund.com.

The author lives in New York and has three other children and five grandsons.